THE
CAMBRIDGE ANCIENT HISTORY

PLATES TO VOLUMES I AND II

THE
CAMBRIDGE
ANCIENT HISTORY

PLATES TO VOLUMES I AND II

NEW EDITION

EDITED BY

I. E. S. EDWARDS F.B.A.

Formerly Keeper of Egyptian Antiquities, The British Museum

THE LATE C. J. GADD

N. G. L. HAMMOND F.B.A.

Professor Emeritus of Greek, University of Bristol

E. SOLLBERGER F.B.A.

Keeper of Western Asiatic Antiquities, The British Museum

CAMBRIDGE UNIVERSITY PRESS

CAMBRIDGE

LONDON · NEW YORK · MELBOURNE

Published by the Syndics of the Cambridge University Press
The Pitt Building, Trumpington Street, Cambridge CB2 1RP
Bentley House, 200 Euston Road, London NW1 2DB
32 East 57th Street, New York, NY 10022, USA
296 Beaconsfield Parade, Middle Park, Melbourne 3206, Australia

© Cambridge University Press 1977

Library of Congress catalogue card number: 75–85719

ISBN 0 521 20571 9

First published 1977

Printed in Great Britain
at the University Press, Cambridge

PREFACE

In the first edition of this History, the initial volume of plates consisted of illustrations to the text of Volumes I–IV. From Volume V onwards one volume of plates was issued with every two volumes of text. This arrangement has been continued in the present edition and this volume supplies the plates for the four parts which comprise Volumes I and II.

In selecting the illustrations for this volume the main considerations have been to exemplify the material on which the arguments in the text are based and to show pieces of particular artistic or technical merit. Documents which contain vital historical evidence may, however, be unsuitable for study when reproduced on a single plate of limited size. Nevertheless, photographs showing either the whole or a part of such documents have been included in the belief that they will be helpful to the student who is not a specialist. A factor which has also been taken into account is the degree of availability and accessibility of other publications in which an object is illustrated. In this respect the task of the Editors has been greatly facilitated by the knowledge that readers can obtain from the footnotes to the text references to periodicals and books mentioned in the bibliographies which will provide adequate descriptions and photographs, particularly of well-known objects and monuments.

The Editors wish to acknowledge the great assistance which they have received from contributors who have not only suggested illustrations for their chapters but also supplied the necessary photographs. No mention is made in the captions of the sources of the photographs, but these particulars will be found in the Contents list at the beginning of the volume. If the source is a museum or other institution it should be understood that the object is now in its collection and thanks are due to the curators and the governing bodies for permission to reproduce the photograph. Above all, the Editors are indebted to the staff of the Cambridge University Press, whose help has extended far beyond providing the technical expertise necessary for the preparation of the volume.

I.E.S.E.
N.G.L.H.
E.S.

CONTENTS

THE DEVELOPMENT OF CITIES FROM AL-'UBAID TO THE END OF URUK 5

SIR MAX MALLOWAN

8 Early Mesopotamian decorated pottery.
   Iraq Museum, Baghdad. *Photo:* Directorate
   General of Antiquities, Baghdad.

PREDYNASTIC EGYPT

ELISE J. BAUMGARTEL

9 Pottery vessels in various styles:
   (*a*) El-Mustagidda.
        British Museum (59721). *Photo:* Museum.
   (*b*)–(*c*) Metropolitan Museum of Art (20.2.10). *Photo*
        Museum.
   (*d*)–(*e*) Naqāda.
        Ashmolean Museum (1895.1220). *Photo:* Museum
   (*f*) Naqāda.
        Ashmolean Museum (1892.482). *Photo:* Museum

10 Knives, pin, chisel, adze and daggers.
   (*a*) British Museum (29289). *Photo:* Museum.
   (*b*) University Museum Manchester (2428). *Photo:*
        Museum.
   (*c*) University College London (5287). *Photo:* College.
   (*d*) Ashmolean Museum (1895.972). *Photo:* Museum.
   (*e*) Cairo Museum. *Photo:* Museum.
   (*f*) Ashmolean Museum (E.3956). *Photo:* Museum.
   (*g*) Cairo Museum (35158). *Photo:* Museum.
   (*h*) Ashmolean Museum (1895.968). *Photo:* Museum.

11 (*a*) Painted pottery figure of a woman. El-Badāri.
        British Museum (59679). *Photo:* Museum.

PALESTINE DURING THE NEOLITHIC AND CHALCOLITHIC PERIODS

R. DE VAUX

CYPRUS IN THE NEOLITHIC AND CHALCOLITHIC PERIODS

H. W. CATLING

THE STONE AGE IN THE AEGEAN

S. S. WEINBERG

THE EARLY DYNASTIC PERIOD IN EGYPT

I. E. S. Edwards

PALESTINE IN THE EARLY BRONZE AGE

R. de Vaux

SYRIA BEFORE 2200 B.C.

Margaret S. Drower

ANATOLIA *c.* 4000–2300 B.C.

J. Mellaart

THE IDENTIFICATION OF TROY

Carl W. Blegen

THE DYNASTY OF AGADE AND THE GUTIAN INVASION
C. J. Gadd

THE MIDDLE KINGDOM IN EGYPT
William C. Hayes

GREECE, CRETE AND THE AEGEAN ISLANDS
IN THE EARLY BRONZE AGE

JOHN L. CASKEY

CYPRUS IN THE EARLY BRONZE AGE

H. W. CATLING

NORTHERN MESOPOTAMIA AND SYRIA
J.-R. Kupper

EGYPT: FROM THE DEATH OF AMMENEMES III TO SEQENENRE II
William C. Hayes

PALESTINE IN THE MIDDLE BRONZE AGE
Kathleen M. Kenyon

GREECE AND THE AEGEAN ISLANDS IN THE MIDDLE BRONZE AGE
John L. Caskey

THE MATURITY OF MINOAN CIVILIZATION
F. Matz

CYPRUS IN THE MIDDLE BRONZE AGE
H. W. Catling

EGYPT: FROM THE EXPULSION OF THE HYKSOS TO AMENOPHIS I

T. G. H. James

EGYPT: INTERNAL AFFAIRS FROM TUTHMOSIS I TO THE DEATH OF AMENOPHIS III

William C. Hayes

SYRIA *c.* 1550–1400 B.C.

MARGARET S. DROWER

PALESTINE IN THE TIME OF THE EIGHTEENTH DYNASTY

Kathleen M. Kenyon

THE ZENITH OF MINOAN CIVILIZATION

F. Matz

THE LINEAR SCRIPTS AND THE TABLETS AS HISTORICAL DOCUMENTS: LITERACY IN MINOAN AND MYCENAEAN LANDS

STERLING DOW

THE RISE OF MYCENAEAN CIVILIZATION

FRANK H. STUBBINGS

TROY VII

Carl W. Blegen

THE EXPANSION OF MYCENAEAN CIVILIZATIOI

Frank H. Stubbings

CYPRUS IN THE LATE BRONZE AGE
H. W. CATLING

EGYPT: FROM THE INCEPTION OF THE NINETEENTH DYNASTY TO THE DEATH OF RAMESSES III
R. O. FAULKNER

ASSYRIAN MILITARY POWER 1300–1200 B.C.

J. M. MUNN-RANKIN

ELAM *c.* 1600–1200 B.C.

RENÉ LABAT

PHRYGIA AND THE PEOPLES OF ANATOLIA IN THE IRON AGE

R. D. Barnett

ASSYRIA AND BABYLONIA *c.* 1200–1000 B.C.

D. J. Wiseman

EGYPT: FROM THE DEATH OF RAMESSES III TO THE END OF THE TWENTY-FIRST DYNASTY

J. ČERNÝ

THE END OF MYCENAEAN CIVILIZATION AND THE DARK AGE: THE ARCHAEOLOGICAL BACKGROUND

V. R. D'A. DESBOROUGH

GREEK SETTLEMENT IN THE EASTERN AEGEAN AND ASIA MINOR

J. M. Cook

177 Fragment of Ionic Geometric vase at Smyrna.
    British School at Athens. *Photo:* British School
    at Athens.

THE RELIGION AND MYTHOLOGY OF THE GREEKS

W. K. C. Guthrie

178 (*a*) Gold ring, showing an altar. Thebes.
    Benaki Museum, Athens. *From* M. Nilsson,
        Geschichte der griechischen Religion III (3rd ed.),
        pl. 19, 2.

    (*b*) Stone receptacle with four depressions in the top.
    Kumasa.
        From ibid. pl. 5, 1.

    (*c*) Offering table. Phaestus.
        Heraklion Museum. *From* ibid. pl. 4, 1.

    (*d*) Double axes on top of *bucrania*. Amphora from Pseira.
        Heraklion Museum. *From* ibid. pl. 8, 1.

    (*e*) Pier with double axes incised on its block. Cnossus.
        From ibid. pl. 9, 3.

179 Snake goddesses: (*a*) faience, (*b*) gold and ivory. Cnossus.
    Heraklion Museum. *From* Nilsson, *Geschichte der*
        griechischen Religion III (3rd ed.), p. 15, 1 and 3.

    (*c*) Sacrificial scene from a sarcophagus. Hagia Triada.
        Heraklion Museum. *From* ibid. pl. 10.

180 (*a*) Model of a shrine with horns of consecration and birds.
    Mycenae.
        National Museum, Athens. *From* Nilsson,
        Geschichte der griechischen Religion III (3rd ed.),
        pl. 7, 1.

    (*b*) Column with horns of consecration and animals; seal-
    impression. Mycenae.
        National Museum, Athens. *From* ibid. pl. 12, 2.

PLATE I

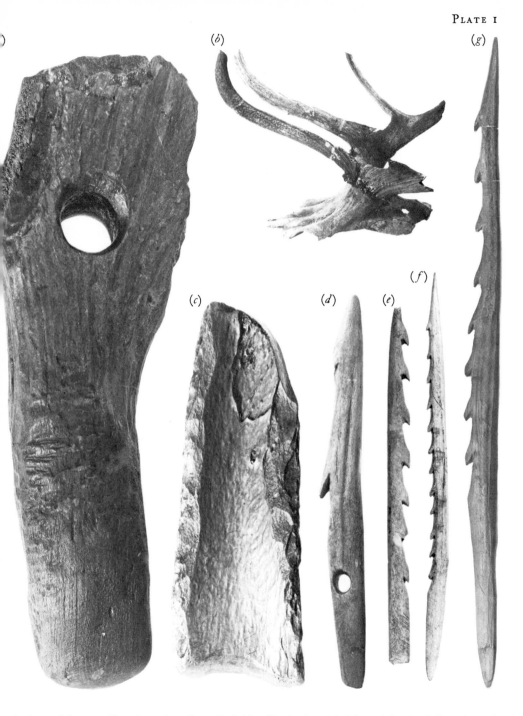

Antler and bone artifacts from Star Carr, Yorkshire, England. (*a*) Mattock-head of elk antler and ·ne (2/3). (*b*) Base of mask made from stag frontlet and antler (1/4). (*c*) Probable leather-working ol of aurochs bone (2/3). (*d*)–(*g*) Barbed spear-heads of stag antler (1/2, 2/3, 1/2, 3/5). (1.1.97)

PLATE 2

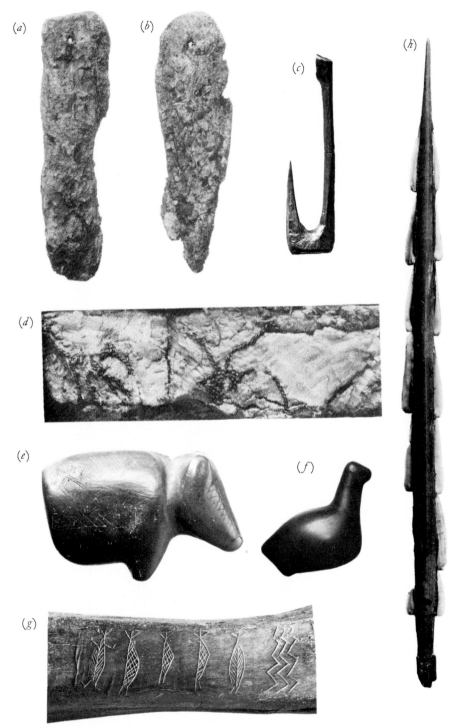

2 Maglemosian (*a*)–(*g*) and Early Coastal (*h*) art and equipment. (*a*)–(*b*) Pine-bark net-floats from Antrea, Finland (*c*. 2/3) (*c*) Bone fish-hook from Sværdborg, Denmark (1/1). (*d*) Remains of fishing net from Antrea, Finland (*c*. 4/5). (*e*)–(*f*) Animal figurines of amber, probably from Denmark (2/3). (*g*) Scene engraved on aurochs bone from Ryemarksgaard, Denmark (1/1). (*h*) Slotted bone point with flint insets from Trorod, Copenhagen (2/3). (1.1.98ff.)

PLATE 3

3 The Sumerian King List: The 'Weld-Blundell Prism' (clay, h. 20 cm) inscribed with the names and length of reigns, with occasional biographical notes, of ante-diluvian kings and of the kings of the first nineteen dynasties 'after the Flood', ending with the Dynasty of Isin. 19th century B.C. Larsa? (I.I.200)

PLATE 4

4   The Assyrian King List: Reverse of the 'Khorsabad King List' (clay, 18 × 13 cm). The list gives the names and length of reigns of 107 kings, from the first 17 'kings who dwelt in tents' (i.e. were tribal chiefs) to Ashur-nirari V (753–746 B.C.). This copy is dated 738 B.C. Khorsabad (Dūr-Sharrukin) (1.1.195)

PLATE 5

5 (*a*) Clay wall relief of a pair of leopards, male and female (1·1 m each). Çatal Hüyük Level VII, *c.* 6200 B.C. (1.1.312)

5 (*b*) Wall painting of a wild-bull hunt. Çatal Hüyük Level V, *c.* 5900 B.C. (1.1.312)

PLATE 8

8 Early Mesopotamian decorated pottery. *Top row*: Hajji Muhammad ware, *c.* 3900–3700 B.C.; *remainder*: Eridu ware,

PLATE 9

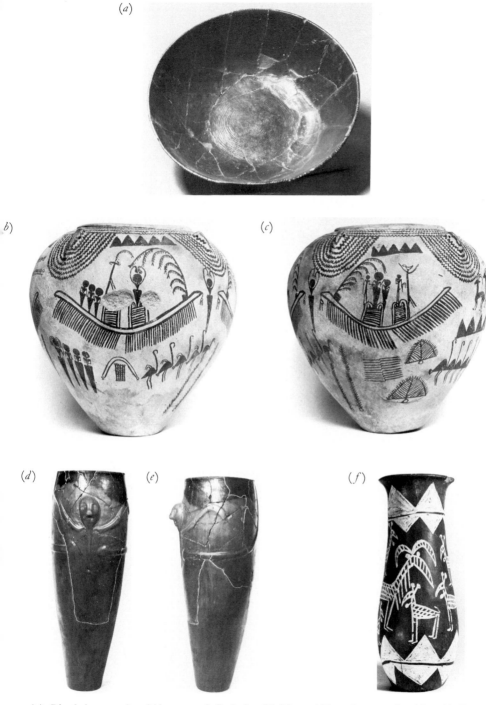

9 (a) Rippled pottery bowl (d. 23·5 cm). Badārian. El-Mustagidda. (1.1.471) (b) & (c) Pottery vase with representations of boats bearing the fertility goddess and her consort (h. 30·0 cm). Naqāda II. Naqāda. (1.1.481, 489) (d) & (e) Black topped pot with an image of the fertility goddess (h. 42·8 cm). Naqāda I. Naqāda. (1.1.480, 493) (f) Red pottery vessel with white cross-lined decoration (h. 25·5 cm). Naqāda I. Naqāda. (1.1.474, 477)

PLATE 10

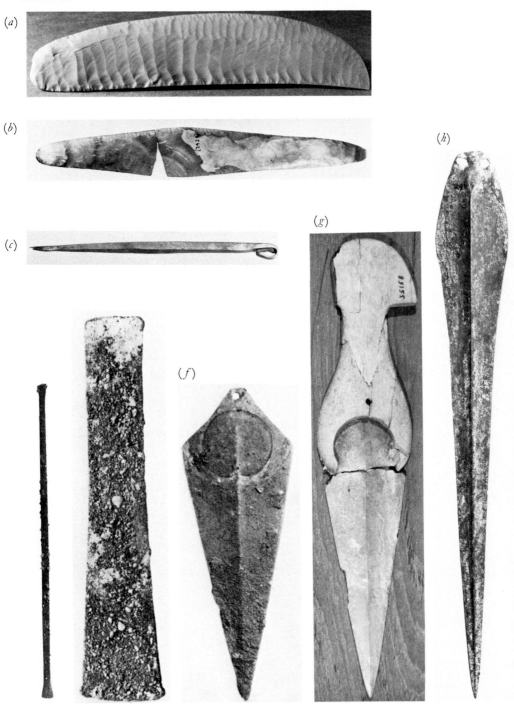

10 (a) Ripple-flaked flint knife (l. 23·5 cm). Naqāda II. Naqāda. (1.1.491) (b) Bifacial flint knife (l. 35 cm). Naqāda I. Naqāda. (1.1.478) (c) Copper pin (l. 9·3 cm). Naqāda I. Naqāda. (1.1.480) (d) Copper chisel (l. 8·3 cm). Naqāda II. Naqāda. (1.1.486) (e) Copper adze (l. 11·7 cm). Naqāda II. Hamra Dōm. (1.1.486) (f) Copper dagger (l. 15·0 cm). Naqāda II. El-Amra. (1.1.486) (g) Silver dagger (l. 12·5 cm). Naqāda II. El-Amra. (1.1.486) (h) Copper dagger (l. 26·5 cm). Naqāda II. Naqāda. (1.1.486)

PLATE 11

11   (*a*) Painted pottery figure of a woman (h. 9·5 cm). Badārian. El-Badāri.   (1.1.491, 494).
(*b*) Clay figure of a woman (h. 13·0 cm). Naqāda I. Abādīya.   (1.1.496)   (*c*) Ivory figure of a
man (h. 35·0 cm). Naqāda I. El-Mahāsna.   (1.1.496)   (*d*) Ivory hippopotamus (l. 8·0 cm).
Badārian. El-Mustagidda.   (1.1.494)   (*e*) Symbol of the fertility goddess (h. 4·9 cm). Naqāda II.
Naqāda.   (1.1.494)

PLATE 12

12 (*a*) Pottery model of a house (l. 46·5 cm). At the opposite end to the door are two windo'
placed high up in the wall. Since the roof is intact the front part of the house seems to have been
open court. Naqāda II. El-Amra. (1.1.484–5)

12 (*b*) Pottery model of a battlemented wall with two sentinels
standing against the inner side (h. 10·5 cm). Naqāda I–II. Abādīya
(1.1.476)

PLATE 13

13 (a) Jericho: the tower (h. 8·50 m) of the Pre-pottery Neolithic A period. 8th millennium B.C.
(1.1.500) (b) Beidha: sandstone houses of Level VI. Pre-pottery Neolithic B, 7th millennium B.C.
(1.1.506)

13 (c) One of ten skulls with the flesh modelled in plaster and the eyes replaced by sea-shells found
in a house of Pre-pottery Neolithic B Jericho. (1.1.504) (d) Pottery figurine of Yarmukian type.
Munḥāṭa, Level IIb. (1.1.515)

PLATE 14

14 (*a*) A hoard of copper objects found in a cave in the Wādi Maḥras (Naḥal Mishmār). Chalcolithic period. (1.1.527).

14 (*b*) Copy of a wall painting. Chalcolithic period. Teleilat Ghassūl, Level IV. (1.1.522)

PLATE 15

15   (*a*) Bone figurine with inlaid eyes. Chalcolithic period. Tell Abu Māṭār.   (1.1.525)
(*b*) Red and grey burnished pottery. Chalcolithic period. Tell el-Fār'ah near Nablus, tomb 3.
(1.1.532)

15   (*c*) Terracotta ossuary in the shape of a house. Chalcolithic period.
'Azor.   (1.1.528)

PLATE 16

(a)

(b)

(c)

(d)

16   Vessels and a statuette from Cyprus.   (a) Decorated stone bowl (l. 30·5 cm) found with burial. Neolithic I. Khirokitia.   (1.1.545)   (b) Spouted bowl (d. 32·5 cm) of combed ware. Neolithic II. Khirokitia.   (1.1.547)   (c) Cruciform stone statuette (h. 15·6 cm). Chalcolithic I. Region of Pomos.   (1.1.554)   (d) Deep jar (h. c. 5·3 cm) of red-on-white ware. Chalcolithic I. Erimi.   (1.1.553)

PLATE 17

17 Bone and stone implements. Aceramic Neolithic. Argissa in Thessaly. (1.1.568)

PLATE 18

18   Early Neolithic site at Nea Nikomedeia in Macedonia.

(*a*) Aerial view of site from the east.   (1.1.577)

(*b*) Steatopygous female figurine of clay from the large central structure, perhaps a shrine. The figurine may represent the 'Mother Goddess'.   (1.1.578)

PLATE 19

19   Early Neolithic site at Nea Nikomedeia in Macedonia (*cont*.).

(*a*) Frogs beautifully modelled in greenstone.   (1.1.580)

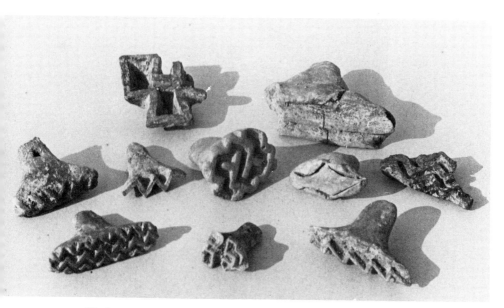

(*b*) Stamp seals of clay with maeandroid pattern.   (1.1.581–2)

PLATE 20

(a)

(b)

(c)

(d)

(e)

20 Neolithic pottery. (a) Painted vase of early style. Early Neolithic. Chaeronea in Boeot
(1.1.585–6) (b) *Ditto* of late style. (1.1.585–6) (c) Urfirnis jug. Middle Neolithic. Lerna
Argolis. (1.1.594) (d) *Ditto* bowl fragment. (1.1.594–5) (e) *Ditto* bowl fragment wi
painted patterns. (1.1.596)

PLATE 21

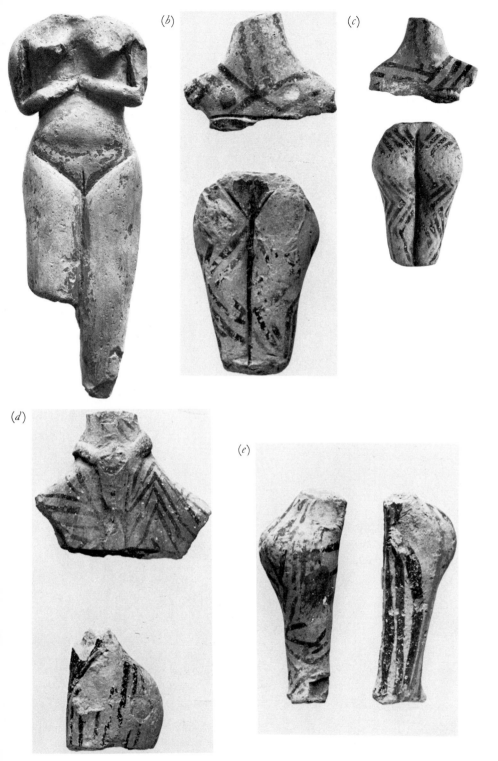

21 Standing female figurines of clay. Middle Neolithic.   (a) With highly burnished red slip.
Lerna.   (b)–(e) With linear patterns and wavy lines in Urfirnis glaze-paint. Lerna and Corinth.
(1.1.596)

PLATE 22

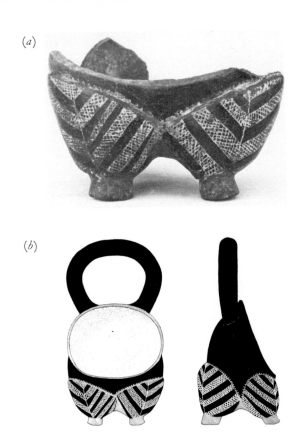

22 Neolithic pottery (*cont.*). (*a*) Fragment of four-legged vase. End of Middle Neolithic. Elatea.
Phocis. (1.1.598) (*b*) Reconstruction of four-legged vase, used for cult purposes. (1.1.59
(*c*) Matt-painted jar on high stand, with face painted on neck. Late Neolithic. Elatea. (1.1.601–
(*d*) Jar with incised rectilinear and spiraliform designs. Late Neolithic. Dhimini in Thessaly. (1.1.60

PLATE 23

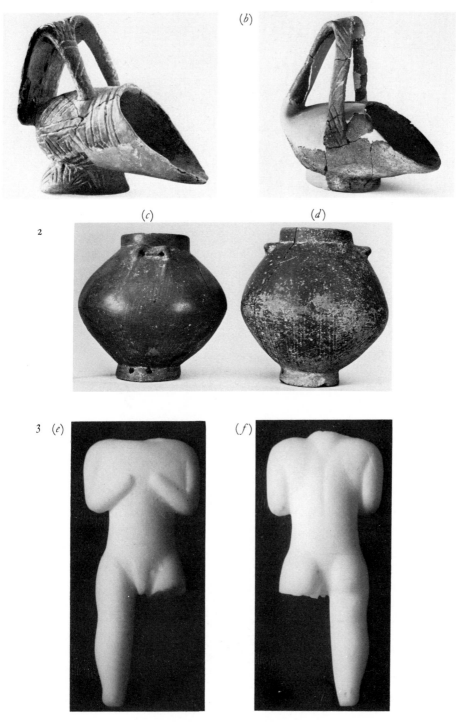

23 (1) Scoop-like incised vessels. Late Neolithic. (a) Sesklo in Thessaly. (1.1.605)
(b) Ceos. (1.1.605) (2) (c)–(d) Jars with white-painted patterns on red-polished
surface. Late Neolithic. Agora of Athens. (1.1.607) (3) (e)–(f) Standing male figure
of white marble. Early Neolithic, Phase I. Cnossus, Stratum VIII. (1.1.610)

PLATE 24

(a)

(b)

(c)

24 Pottery of Early Neolithic, Phase I. Cnossus, from pits in Stratum VIII. (1.1.610)

PLATE 25

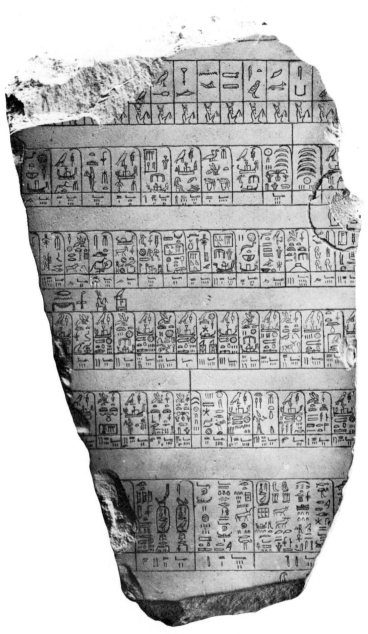

25   Cast of the Palermo Stone (*recto*). The top line gives the names of predy-
nastic kings. Lines 2–5 refer to events in the Early Dynastic Period and in the
first five years of the 3rd Dynasty. The bottom line records events in the reign of
King Sneferu (first king of the 4th Dynasty). 5th Dynasty, *c.* 2450 B.C.   (*See*
General Indexes, 1.1.730 and 1.2.1043)

PLATE 26

26 The Abydos king-list. The uppermost and the middle rows of cartouches contain the names of kings in chronological order, beginning with Menes and ending with Sethos I. In the bottom line the names of Sethos I are repeated. 19th Dynasty, c. 1310 B.C. Temple of Sethos I at Abydos. (*See* General Indexes, I.1.679 and I.2.1013)

PLATE 27

27 Columns 3–5 of the Turin canon. The fragmentary remains of entries in these columns record the names of kings from the 2nd to the 12th Dynasties and the length of each reign. 19th Dynasty, Ramesses II, c. 1250 B.C. (See General Indexes, 1.1.752 and 1.2.1055)

PLATE 28

(a)

(b)

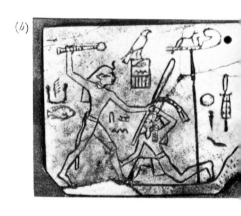

(c)

28 (a) Red granite stela inscribed with the Horus-name of Reneb (h. 99·0 cm). 2nd Dynasty
c. 2850 B.C. Probably Saqqara. (1.2.30) (b) Ivory docket showing Den smiting an Eastern
with a mace (w. 5·4 cm). 1st Dynasty, c. 3000 B.C. Abydos. (1.2.27) (c) Limestone tria
piece showing two figures of a king in *Sed*-festival dress, birds and a baboon (w. 39·3 cm). I
Dynasty, c. 3000 B.C. Saqqara. (1.2.21)

PLATE 29

(b)

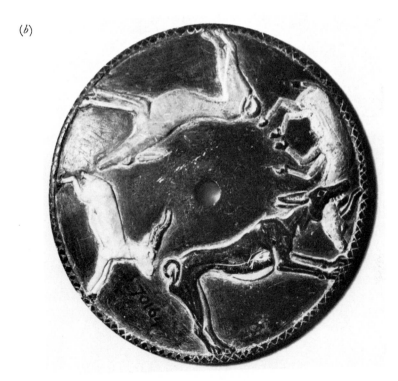

29 (a) Conjectural reconstruction of a brick mastaba dated to the time of Queen Mer(it)neith
(l. 42·5 m). 1st Dynasty, c. 3000 B.C. Saqqara. (1.2.61) (b) Black steatite disk inlaid with
coloured stones showing hounds hunting gazelles (d. 8·7 cm). 1st Dynasty, c. 3000 B.C. Saqqara.
(1.2.69)

PLATE 30

30 (a) The 'Overseer' Ebikh-il. Alabaster, eyes of shell and lapis lazuli set in bitumen; inscribed (h. 52·5 cm). Early Dynastic III*b*. Mari (temple of Ishtar). (1.2.115, 295)

30 (b) Limestone plaque (h. 32 cm). The top register picts a banquet scene; the lower registers show attend bringing the materials of the feast. Early Dynastic Khafājī. (1.2.135f.)

30 (c) Inlaid shell figures. (The restoration of the first figure in the bottom row as a standard bear is incorrect: the 'standard' is actually a rein-ring, and its shaft a length of rope.) Early Dynastic III Mari (temple of Ishtar). (1.2.121, 295)

PLATE 31

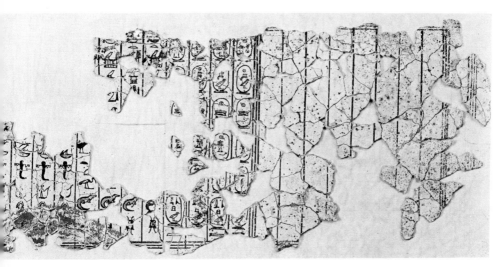

31 (*a*) Wooden board overlaid with plaster on which are written names of early kings. 5th Dynasty, *c.* 2450 B.C. Giza (Western cemetery, tomb G. 1011).   (I.2.30, 150, 205)

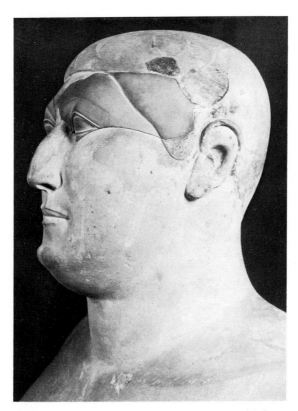

31 (*b*) Head of a seated limestone statue of Prince Hemiunu (h. of statue 1·56 m). 4th Dynasty, *c.* 2580 B.C. Giza.   (I.2.166, 206)

PLATE 32

32 (*a*) The Queens' pyramids and the royal cemetery on the east side of the pyramid of Cheops. 4th Dynasty, *c.* 2580 B.C. Giza. (1.2.169)

32 (*b*) Painted reliefs in the rock-cut tomb of Queen Meresankh III, wife of Chephren. The queen is shown in the centre, her mother, Hetepheres II, on her right and her son, Nebemakhet, on her left. 4th Dynasty, *c.* 2500 B.C. Giza. (1.2.175)

PLATE 33

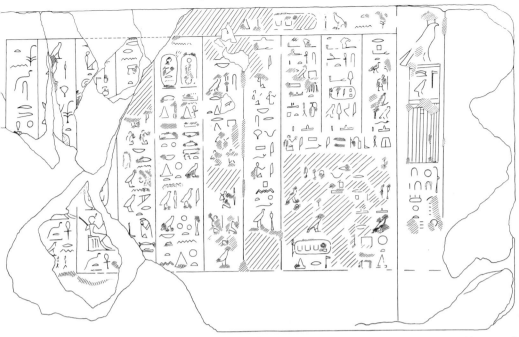

a) Decree dated to the sixty-first year of the reign of Phiops II. Its contents refer to the pyramid-town of rinus. 6th Dynasty, *c.* 2200 B.C. Giza (Temple of Mycerinus).   (I.2.195–6)

33   (*b*) Painted limestone relief showing bears and a Syrian vase. 5th Dynasty, *c.* 2480 B.C. Abusīr (Temple of Sahure).   (I.2.183, 350)

PLATE 34

(a)

(b)

34 (a) Tell el-Fārʿah: the city-gate, looking to the entrance into the town. Early Bronze I*b*.
(1.2.216f.) (b) Tell el-Fārʿah: the Early Bronze strata (mostly I*b*), looking to the north-
east. *In the foreground:* a street leading to the rampart bordered by houses, and the sanctuary.
Top left: stone rampart of Early Bronze II. (1.2.217)

PLATE 35

(a)

(b)

35 (a) 'Ai: the main hall of the 'palace', seen from the north. Early Bronze III. (1.2.221) (b) 'Ai: last stage of the sanctuary, seen from the north-east. *From left to right:* the entrance hall, the cult-room with a dais (*bottom*), and the cella with the altar (*top*). Early Bronze III. (1.2.221f.)

PLATE 36

(a)

(b)

36 (a) Megiddo: the sanctuary of Levels XVIII–XVI, looking south. The round structure is an altar, the first example of a *bāmāh*. Early Bronze III. (1.2.222f.) (b) Bāb ed-Draʻ: the funerary building A 21 after removal of most of the bone piles. Early Bronze II–III. (1.2.225)

PLATE 37

(a)

(b)

37 (a) Tell el-Fār'ah: pottery kiln; it has two chambers separated by a sleeper supported by a pillar and pierced with flues, the lower chamber for the fire, the upper one for stacking the pots. End of Early Bronze I. (1.2.227) (b) Kirbet Karak: detail of large building showing the platform and one of the paved circles containing four low projections. Early Bronze III. (1.2.229f.)

PLATE 38

(a)

(c)

(b)

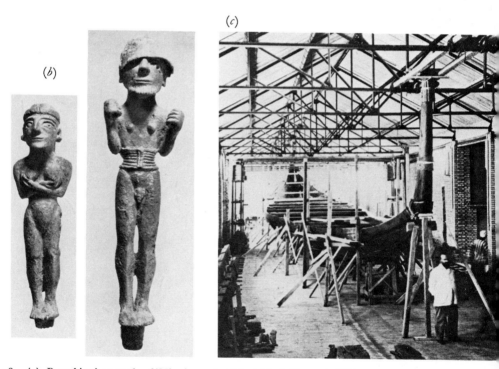

38   (a) Baetyl in the temple of 'Ninni-zaza' at Mari. Early Dynastic IIIb.   (1.2.329)   (b) Female a
male copper figurines of worshippers (h. 13 and 17 cm). Early Bronze I–II. Tell Judaidah.   (1.2.34
(c) Funerary boat of Cheops (l. 42·65 m) reassembled. 4th Dynasty, c. 2580 B.C. Giza.   (1.2.347)

PLATE 39

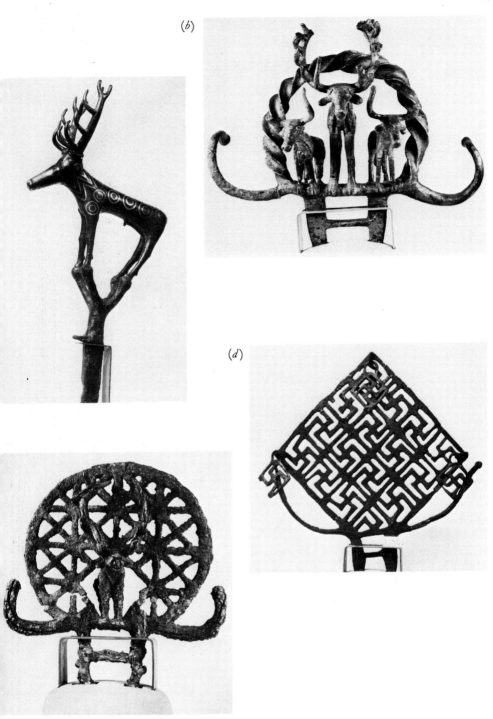

(b)

(d)

9 (a) Figure of a stag (h. 52 cm), copper with gold plating and electrum inlays. Early Bronze II.
laca Hüyük.   (1.2.391)   (b)–(d) Copper 'standards': (b) with figures of stag and bulls (h. 22 cm);
) with figure of bull and geometric pattern (h. 19 cm); (d) with geometric pattern (h. 32 cm).
arly Bronze II. Alaca Hüyük.   (1.2.391)

PLATE 40

(b)

(c)

40 (a) Gold drinking-cup (h. 13 cm). Early Bronze II. Alaca Hüyük. (1.2.394) (b) Wall and tower of the small fortress known as Troy I, seen from the south-west. (1.2.413) (c) The mound of Hisarlik, identified with Troy, seen from the north. (1.2.411)

PLATE 41

41   (*a*) Limestone stela with representation of a human face. Early Bronze Age. Troy I. (1.2.413)   (*b*) Cuneiform tablet: letter from a man striving to restore his farm amid the attacks of the Gutians. Reign of Shar-kali-sharri, 2217–2193 B.C.   (1.2.450, 456)   (*c*) Cuneiform tablet: list of provisions, trees and wooden objects. *c.* 2270 B.C.   (1.2.450)

PLATE 42

(a)

(c)

42   (a) Victory stela (pink sandstone, h. 2 m) of Naram-Sin (2254–2218 B.C.) picturing his triumph ove
the king of Lullubi. Susa.   (1.2.443)   (b) Alabaster statuette (h. 46 cm) of Ur-Ningirsu, son of Gude
of Lagash. The relief on the base shows men carrying offerings. c. 2150 B.C.   (1.2.460)   (c) 'Indu
Valley'-type stamp seals. The square one (view of back of original and modern impression of face, 27 ⨉
23 mm) bears a cuneiform inscription; the round ones (modern impressions, d. 25, 31 and 22 mm) ar
inscribed in the Indus script. Agade period, 24th–23rd centuries B.C. Ur (2, 4), Babylonia (1, 3
(1.2.453)

PLATE 43

43 (*a*) Impressions of cylinder seals of the Agade period showing religious ceremonies (1: h. 32 mm, d. 20 mm; 2: h. 26 mm,
d. 15 mm; 3: h. 35 mm, d. 22 mm), *c.* 2270 B.C. (I.2.451)

43 (*b*) Painted wooden model with representations of Egyptian soldiers carrying spears, copper-
tipped lances and leather shields (l. 1·93 m). 9th–10th Dynasties, *c.* 2130 B.C. Asyūt. (I.2.469)

PLATE 44

44 Biographical stela of the Chancellor Tjetji, who held office under Wahankh and Nakhtnebtep-
nefer. In the lower register, behind the large figure of Tjetji, are representations of his Treasurer,
Megegi, and his Companion, Tjeru (h. 1·5 m). 11th Dynasty, c. 2065 B.C. Dirā Abu'n-Naga.
(1.2.477)

PLATE 45

(a)

45   (a) Black granite statue of Sesostris III (h. 1·35 m). 12th Dynasty, c. 1860 B.C. Deir el-Bahri (Temple of Nebhepetre Mentuhotpe II).   (1.2.505)   (b) Festival pavilion of Sesostris I. 12th Dynasty, c. 1950 B.C. Karnak.   (1.2.502)

PLATE 46

(a)   (b)

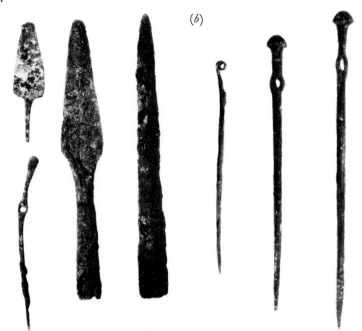

(c)

46 (a) Bronze toggle-pin and wea-
pons. Early Bronze–Middle Bronze
period. Megiddo (tomb 1101 B).
(1.2.579) (b) Bronze toggle-pins.
Early Bronze–Middle Bronze period.
Megiddo (shaft tombs). (1.2.581)
(c) Bronze toggle-pin, beads and brace-
lets. Early Bronze–Middle Bronze
period. Ras Shamra (tomb LXI).
(1.2.585)

PLATE 47

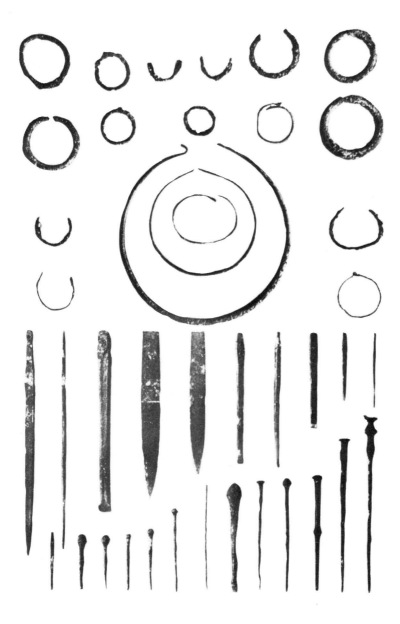

47 Torcs and other bronze objects from a temple-offering deposit placed in a jar (no. 2132) at Byblos. (1.2.588ff.)

PLATE 48

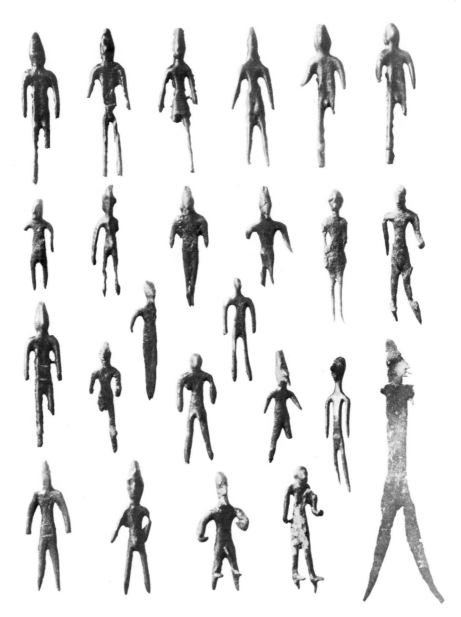

48 Bronze figurines from a temple-offering deposit placed in a jar (no. 2000) at Byblos. (1.2.588ff.)

PLATE 49

(c)

49 (a) Ur: the north-west staircase of the zikkurrat. Time of Ur-Nammu, 2113–2096 B.C. (1.2.599)
(b) Scenes from a sculptured stone stela (h. 3 m) descriptive of Ur-Nammu's building of the temple of
the Moon-god. 2113–2096 B.C. Ur. (1.2.599,628) (c) Inscribed alabaster slab (h. 53 cm) recording
Shu-Sin's repulse of an Amorite raid and his building of the temple of Shara at Umma. 2030 B.C.
Umma. (1.2.609f.)

PLATE 50

(a)

(b)

(c)

50 (a) Ur: entrance to the tomb of King Shulgi (2095–2048 B.C.). (1.2.607) (b) Hurrian founda-tion deposit. Bronze lion (h. 12·2 cm) and stone tablet (12·2 × 8·5 cm) inscribed in Hurrian by Tisari (or: Tisatal), king of Urkish. Agade period (24th–23rd centuries B.C.). 'Amuda, N. Syria. (1.2.624f.) (c) Bronze plaque (15 × 11·7 cm) inscribed in Akkadian by the Hurrian king Arisen (or: Atalsen) of Urkish and Nawar. Agade period (24th–23rd centuries B.C.). Samarra (?). (1.2.624f.)

PLATE 51

51 (*a*) Dolerite statue (h. 88 cm) of a ruler, probably of Eshnunna. *c.* 2000 B.C. Susa. (I.2.629)
(*b*) Seal impression on a clay bulla (l. 5·5 cm): King Ibbi-Sin (2029–2006 B.C.) making a presentation
to one of his officials. Nippur. (I.2.630) (*c*) Bronze foundation figurine (h. 28 cm) of Ur-Nammu
(2113–2096 B.C.). Uruk. (I.2.631)

PLATE 52

(a)

(b)　　　　(c)

52　(a) Fragment (h. 50 cm) of a stone stela of Sargon of Agade (2371–2316 B.C.). *Top row:* prisoners of war; *bottom row:* the king (identified by an inscription) at the head of his troops. Susa.　(1.2.433; 648f.)　(b) Fragment (h. 14·6 cm) of an alabaster figure of the Elamite king Kutik (*or:* Puzur)-In-Shushinak (c. 2240 B.C.), with an Akkadian inscription. Susa. (1.2.652)　(c) Limestone statue (h. 84 cm) of the Elamite goddess Narundi, with an inscription of Kutik-In-Shushinak in Elamite and Akkadian. c. 2240 B.C. Susa.　(1.2.669)

PLATE 53

(*a*)

(*c*)

3 (*a*) Limestone relief (h. 57 cm) showing the Elamite god In-Shushinak supporting a peg of bronze nd cedar wood before the figure of a lion. Behind him stands a goddess, probably Narundi. Inscribed in lamite and Akkadian by Kutik-In-Shushinak, *c.* 2240 B.C. Susa. (1.2.675) (*b*) Kurāngān: rock lief showing a god sitting on a serpent-throne and pouring a libation. *c.* 2150 B.C. (1.2.673) (*c*) Ku-ngān: rock relief showing worshipper on steps approaching the main group, *c.* 2150 B.C. (1.2.673)

PLATE 54

(a)

(b)

(c)

54   (a) Gold jug (h. 42 cm), c. 2200 B.C. Mahmatlar. (I.2.686)   (b)–(c) Cappadocian painted p[?]tery: storage jars (h. 97 and 93 cm) c. 2100 B.C. Kültepe. (I.2.687)

PLATE 55

(a)

(b)

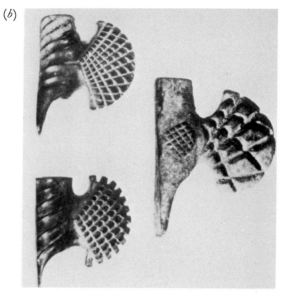

(c)

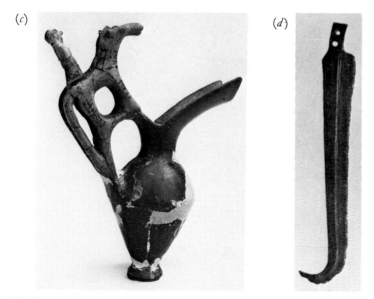

(d)

55 (a) Copper statuette (h. 21·5 cm) of naked woman suckling her child. c. 2200 B.C. Horoztepe. (1.2.690) (b) Bronze crescentic axeheads. c. 2200 B.C. Horoztepe. (1.2.691) (c) Spouted jug with handle in form of horse and rider. c. 2000 B.C. Kültepe, kārum Level II. (1.2.687) (d) Bronze knife with curling tip (l. 20 cm). c. 2100 B.C. Denizli. (1.2.699)

4

PLATE 56

(a)

(b)

(c)

(d)

56 (a) Grey-brown bowl. Sub-Neolithic. Eutresis in Boeotia. (1.2.778) (b) Red burnished-
jug. Early Helladic I. Eutresis. (1.2.778) (c) Gold sauceboat. Early Helladic II. Western Arca
(1.2.789) (d) Pottery sauceboat. Early Helladic II. Lerna III. (1.2.785)

PLATE 57

(b)

57 (a) and (b) Glazed pottery saucers. Early Helladic II. Eutresis. (1.2.779)

(c) Typical site of an Early Helladic village. Promontory at Kaki Thalassa, Attica. (1.2.781)

PLATE 58

(a)

(b)

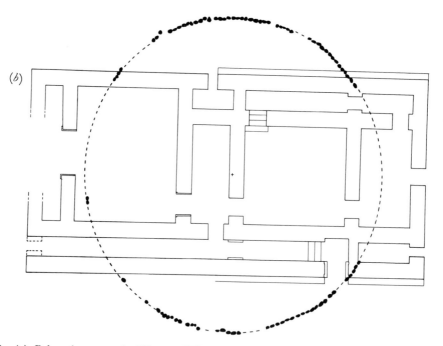

58 (a) Palace, known as the 'House of Tiles' (c. 12 × 25 m), inside a fortified citadel. Early Hella
II. Lerna III. (1.2.784) (b) Low tumulus of soil (d. c. 19 m) bordered by a ring of stones, over
debris of the 'House of Tiles'. Lerna III/IV. (1.2.785)

PLATE 59

(a)

(a) Pottery tankard, decorated in white paint on a dark ground. Early Helladic III. Lerna IV.
2.779)   (b) Pottery jar, decorated in dark paint on a light ground. Early Helladic III. Lerna IV.
2.779)

PLATE 60

(a)

(b)

(c)

60 Pots and artifacts of Lerna in Argolis. Early Helladic III. Lerna IV. (a) Pottery cups
(b) grey pottery bowl. (1.2.786) (c) Terracotta double hook or 'anchor'. (1. 2.774, 786)

PLATE 61

(a)

61 Pottery from the Cyclades. (a) Sauceboat, decorated in lustrous dark paint on a light ground. Early Cycladic II. Naxos. (1.2.796) (b) Dark-coloured burnished jar. Early Cycladic II. Syros. (1.2.798)

PLATE 62

(a)

(b)

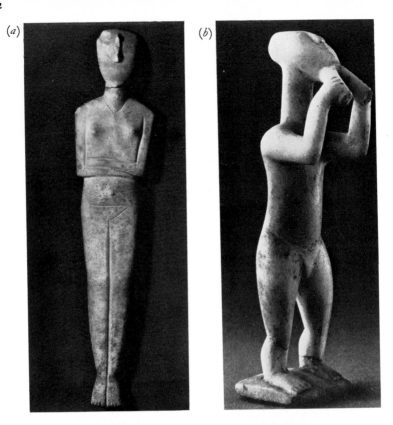

(c)

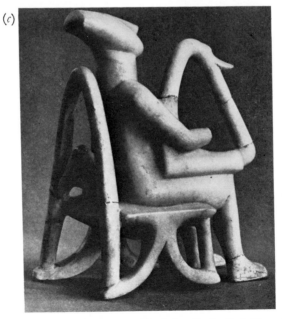

62 Figurines in marble from the Cyclades. Early Cycladic. (1.2.798)
(a) Naturalistic but highly stylized figurine. (b) Figurine representing a
flute player. Keros. (c) Figurine representing a harpist. Keros.

PLATE 63

(b)

(d)

63   Pottery from Crete.   (a) Tall chalice, decorated with burnished patterns. Sub-Neolithic. Pyrgos.
(1.2.801) (b) Jug decorated in red-brown paint on a light ground. Early Minoan I. Ayios Onou-
phrios. (1.2.801) (c) Jug decorated in dull white paint on a lustrous black slip. Early Minoan
III. Mochlos. (d) Red-brown mottled jug. Early Minoan II. Vasiliki. (1.2.802)

PLATE 64

(a)

(b)   (c)

64   (a) Terracotta model of an open-air sanctuary, found in a tomb. Early Cypriot III. Bellapa(is)
(1.2.817)   (b) Red polished-ware jug (Philia stage), with flat base, tall neck and cut-away mout(h).
Early Cypriot I. Philia.   (1.2.812)   (c) 'Plank-shaped' terracotta statuette of red polished-ware. Ear(ly)
Cypriot III.   (1.2.819)

PLATE 65

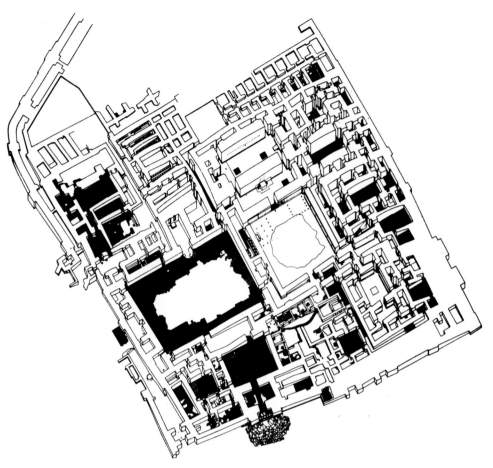

65   Mari: axonometric perspective of the Palace. 18th century B.C.   (II.I.IIf.)

PLATE 66

66 Central panel of the 'Investiture Painting', a large fresco (2·50 × 1·75 m) in courtyard 106 of the Palace of Mari. *Upper register:* the king (Zimrilim?) receives the insignia of power from the goddess Ishtar; *lower register:* goddesses with 'flowing vases'. 18th century B.C. (II.1.12)

PLATE 67

67 (*a*) Specimen of fresco from the Level VII palace at Alalakh. Late
18th–early 17th centuries B.C. (II.I.33)

67 (*b*) Alalakh: the Level VII city-gate, general view of the gateway from
the inside. Late 18th–early 17th centuries B.C. (II.I.33)

PLATE 68

(a)

(b)

(c)

(d)

(e)

(f)

68 Impressions from cylinder seals in the so-called 'Syrian style' (a: h. 26 mm, d. 10 mm; b: h. 23 mm, d. 10 mm; c: h. 22 mm, d. 10 mm; d: h. 12 mm, d. 18 mm; e: h. 23 mm, d. 11 mm; f: h. 21·5 mm, d. 11 mm). 2nd quarter of 2nd millennium B.C. (II.1.40)

PLATE 69

69   Title-page of the Rhind Mathematical Papyrus, a document copied by a scribe named Ahmose from a 'writing of antiquity' in the thirty-third year of Auserre Apophis I. The historical details are written in three vertical columns on the right-hand side. The main text consists of a table setting out the division of 2 by odd numbers to 101 and eighty-four arithmetical problems with their solutions (l. of entire papyrus 5·25 m). 15th Dynasty, c. 1580 B.C. (II. I. 61-2)

PLATE 70

70 Wooden statue of King Awibre Hor (h. 1·77 m). Originally it was covered with a greyish pai[n]
and an apron was suspended from a girdle around the waist. Each hand held a sceptre. The arms abov[e]
the head show that the statue symbolizes the *ka* (spirit or double) of the king. His tomb lay within t[he]
pyramid-enclosure of Ammenemes III, a location which suggests a family connection. 13th Dynast[y,]
c. 1750 B.C. Dahshur. (II.1.46)

PLATE 71

(*a*)

(*b*)

71 (*a*) Green schist statuette of Meryankhre Mentuhotpe (h. 22 cm) formerly in the collection of the Duke of Northumberland. 13th Dynasty, *c*. 1700 B.C. Karnak. (II.1.53). (*b*) Bronze dagger of an official of Nebkhepeshre Apophis III named Nehmen (1·35 cm). The wooden hilt, overlaid with electrum, shows Nehmen thrusting a spear into a lion which is attacking an antelope. 16th Dynasty, *c*. 1570 B.C. Saqqara. (II.1.64)

PLATE 72

72 (a) Jericho (Trench I): the Middle Bronze II rampart with plastered face. (II.1.91f.)

72 (b) Jericho (Trench II): section through the Middle Bronze II rampart.

PLATE 73

73 Aerial view of the site of Hazor.

PLATE 74

74 Middle Helladic pottery from Lerna in Argolis. (II.I.119)

(*a*) Grey Minyan kantharos.

(*b*) Matt-painted cup.

(*c*) Matt-painted kantharos.

PLATE 75

75 Middle Helladic pottery from Lerna (*cont.*). (II.I.120)

(*a*) Matt-painted barrel-jar.

(*b*) Jar with pattern in lustrous dark paint on a light ground.

PLATE 76

(a)

(b)

(c)

76 (a) Bored stone hammer-axe. Early Helladic III. Lerna. (b) Flask in hand-made black burni
ware with incised pattern. Middle Helladic. Lerna. (c) Spouted jar imported from Crete (M.M
M.M. IIa). From Middle Helladic grave, Lerna.

PLATE 77

(a)

(b)

7   Middle Cycladic pottery.   (II . I . 129)   (a) Jar with decoration in semi-lustrous paint. Provenance
ncertain.   (b) Barrel-jar with decoration in dull paint. Phylakopi.

PLATE 78

(a)

(b)

78   (a) Middle Helladic houses at Lerna.   (b) Middle Helladic grave, Lerna.   (II.1.134)

PLATE 79

79 Tomb group containing a Middle Minoan II vase. Abydos, Egypt. (II.1.143)

PLATE 80

80 The palace at Phaestus in Crete. (II.I.147) (*a*) The central court, looking north.

80 (*b*) The west entrance.

PLATE 81

81   Painted pottery of the Middle Minoan period in Crete.   (II.1.153)   (a)–(g) Middle
Minoan I.   (h) Middle Minoan II.

PLATE 82

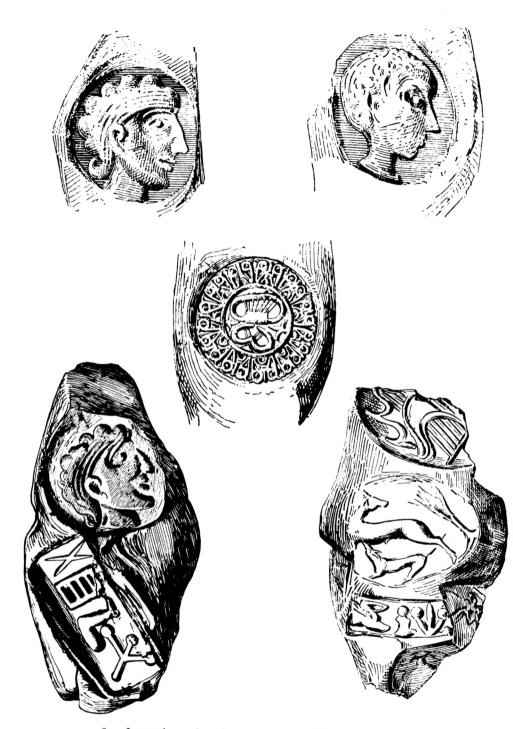

82   Impressions taken from seals in the 'Hieroglyphic Deposit' at
Cnossus in Crete.   (II.1.157)

PLATE 83

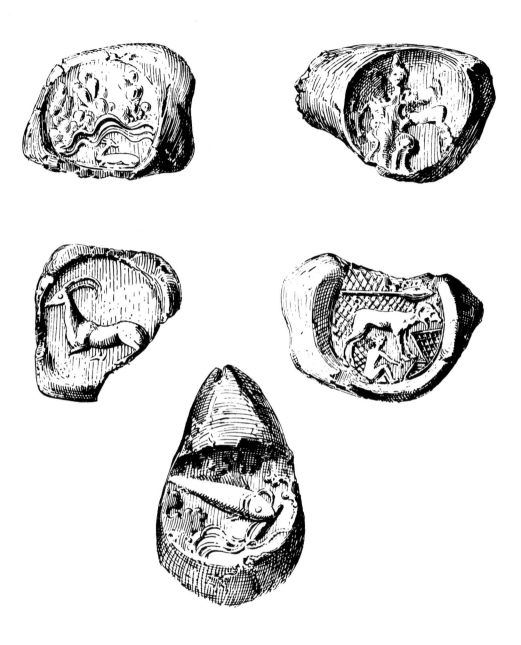

83   Impressions taken from seals in the 'Hieroglyphic Deposit' *cont.*

PLATE 84

84 Jug of White Painted II Ware. Middle Cypriot I. Provenance unknown. (II.1.172)

PLATE 85

85 Jug of Red-on-Black Ware. Middle Cypriot III. Probably from the Karpass. (II.I.172)

PLATE 86

86 Painted limestone statuette of Queen Tetisheri (h. 37 cm). Her headdress is in the form of a
vulture with pendent wings; the head of the bird, which was made of metal, is missing. Although she is
represented as a young woman it is possible that the statuette was not made until after her death in the
reign of her grandson, Amosis I. 17th–18th Dynasties, c. 1570 B.C. Thebes. (II.1.306)

PLATE 87

87 Limestone statue of Queen Hatshepsut (h. 1·96 m). Although the headdress and kilt are those of a king, the body is that of a female and the sensitive carving of the face suggests that it is an idealized portrait of the queen. The head, forearms and part of the throne were found in 1926–8 in excavations conducted by the Metropolitan Museum of Art and the remainder in 1845 by Richard Lepsius. 18th Dynasty, c. 1490 B.C. Deir el-Bahri. (II.1.407)

PLATE 88

88 Yellow quartzite sarcophagus of Tuthmosis I (l. 2·50 m) mounted on a (partly destroyed) alabaster base. According to the inscription carved in the elongated cartouche above the funerary texts, the sarcophagus was made by his son, Tuthmosis II, who is, however, not mentioned by name. Some years after his death, the body of Tuthmosis I was transferred by Hatshepsut to her tomb

PLATE 89

89 Religious scenes on a red quartzite shrine of Queen Hatshepsut. The queen, clad in the attire of a king and wearing the ceremonial beard, stands before the bark of Amun which nine priests carry on their shoulders. Between the queen and the bark are small representations of shrines mounted on sledges. Behind the queen stands Tuthmosis III burning incense. Below are personifications of royal estates bearing offerings. 18th Dynasty, c. 1490 B.C. Karnak. (II.1.331)

PLATE 90

90   Painted limestone head of an Osiride statue of Hatshepsut (h. 1·25 m approx.). On her head is the Double Crown of Upper and Lower Egypt and the beard of Osiris is attached to her chin. When complete, the statue measured about 3·7 m in height. It was placed with others of a similar kind in one of the niches in the uppermost court of the queen's temple at Deir el-Bahri. 18th Dynasty, c. 1490 B.C.   (11.1.409)

PLATE 91

91 Painted limestone head of an Osiride statue of Hatshepsut, a companion piece to the one shown on Pl. 90 and approximately of the same size. In this piece the face is reddish yellow and the headdress is the crown of Upper Egypt. Both the statues have naturalistic features which are suggestive of those of the queen. 18th Dynasty, *c.* 1490 B.C. Deir el-Bahri. (II.I.409)

PLATE 92

92 Black granite block-statue of Sennefer, Chancellor and Superintendent of the Palace in the time of Hatshepsut or Tuthmosis III (h. 87 cm). The inscription begins with a prayer to Osiris for funerary offerings, continues with a list of the deceased's achievements and the official positions which he had held in his lifetime, and ends with a claim for a blissful afterlife. 18th Dynasty, c. 1490 B.C. Thebes. (II.1.411)

PLATE 93

93 Black granite statuette of the Chief Steward Senenmut with the Princess Neferure seated on his lap (h. 71 cm). The princess is represented wearing the side-lock character-istic of children and a ceremonial beard after the fashion of her mother, Hatshepsut (*see* Pl. 89). The statuette, which is one of a small group of its kind, is intended to symbolize the influential position occupied by Senenmut in the queen's household. 18th Dynasty, *c.* 1490 B.C. Thebes. (11.1.412)

PLATE 94

(a)

(b)

94 (a) Upper part of a schist statue of Tuthmosis III (h. of statue 2 m). Artistically it is outstanding and the facial features suggest that it is an idealized portrait of the king. 18th Dynasty, c. 1475 B. Karnak. (II.I.407–8) (b) Head of a colossal breccia seated statue of Amenophis III (h. 1·17 m The elongation of the face, emphasized by the downward angle of the eyes, is a sculptural innovatio 18th Dynasty, c. 1400 B.C. Thebes. (II.I.408)

PLATE 95

(a)

(b)

95 (a) Pink granite relief showing Amenophis II in a chariot shooting arrows through
a tree-trunk and a copper target. 18th Dynasty, c. 1440 B.C. Karnak. (II.1.335)
(b) Front of a chariot of Tuthmosis IV made of wood and overlaid with gilded gesso.
On each side of the king's name are scenes of fierce battles between Egyptians and
Asiatics. Beneath is the symbol of the uniting of Upper and Lower Egypt to which Asiatics
are tied. 18th Dynasty, c. 1420 B.C. Thebes. (II.1.410, 415)

PLATE 96

96 Wall-painting from the tomb of the Scribe of the Royal Estates, Menna. Standing in a boat made of stems of papyrus lashed together, Menna is in the act of hurling a throw-stick (others are just reaching the target) at pin-tail ducks rising from a papyrus thicket. His wife stands behind him and his daughter kneels to pick a lotus bud from the water. In the lower register servants are shown bringing offerings to the tomb. 18th Dynasty, c. 1420 B.C. Thebes. (II.1.413)

PLATE 97

7 Wall-relief from the tomb of the Vizier Ramose. The person portrayed is a member of the house-
old staff of the vizier whose name is not recorded in this scene. In spite of its formality the purity of line
nd delicate modelling of the face and body give it distinction as a work of art. An unusual feature is that
he eyes are not carved but painted. 18th Dynasty, c. 1380 B.C. Thebes. (II.1.342, 417)

PLATE 98

(a)

(b)

98 (a) Idrimi, king of Alalakh. Limestone statue (h. 1·04 m) on basalt throne (h. 66 cm), decora
with lions in relief on the sides. 2nd half of 16th century B.C. Açana. (II.1.435, 524) (b) Tuthm
III smites Asiatic prisoners who hold up their arms begging for mercy. Behind and beneath the prison
are carved the names of places in Palestine and Syria. 18th Dynasty, c. 1475 B.C. Karnak. (II.1.4
452)

PLATE 99

99 (*a*) Wall painting from the tomb of Menkheperreseneb showing foreigners bringing gifts to Tuthmosis III. According to the legend the first three figures represent princes of Keftiu, Kheta and Tunip,
but the first at least is wrongly identified. The fourth is a Keftiuan carrying a large bull's head rhyton.
18th Dynasty, *c.* 1475 B.C. Thebes. (II.1.470, 511) (*b*) Suppliant foreigner before an envoy of
General (later King) Horemheb (h. 50 cm). 18th Dynasty, *c.* 1355 B.C. Saqqara. (II.1.469, 512)

PLATE 100

100 Stone stela (h. 1·42 m) depicting the Thunder god
of Ugarit. 13th century B.C. Ras Shamra. (II.1.476)

PLATE 101

101   Stela showing Amenemope, a builder, adoring Mekal (h. 28·3 cm). Behind Amenemope is his
son Pareemheb. 18th Dynasty, c. 1450 B.C. Beth-shan.   (II.1.476)

PLATE 102

(a)

(b)

102 (a) Limestone stela of a Syrian spearman (h. 30 cm). The owner, with his spear behind him, sits drinking beer through a tube, assisted by his son. His wife sits in front of him. Amarna period, c. 1370 B.C. (II.1.482) (b) Seal of Saustatar, king of Mitanni (c. 1500–1450 B.C.); plastic reconstruction from an impression on a cuneiform tablet. Yorghan Tepe. (II.1.433, 523)

PLATE 103

103 (*a*) Bronze tablet (11 × 15·5 cm) with inscription in Byblite syllabic linear script. 2nd millennium B.C. Byblos. (II.1.517)

103 (*b*) Wall-painting depicting Syrian emissaries bringing gifts to the Egyptian court (h. 114 cm). 18th Dynasty, *c.* 1420 B.C. Thebes (tomb of Sobkhotpe). (II.1.512)

PLATE 104

104   Ugarit: postern gate and glacis.

PLATE 105

(c)

(b)

105 (a) Boar's head axe: copper socket inlaid with gold, and iron blade (l. 19·5 cm). Late 15th century B.C. Ras Shamra. (II.I.513) (b)–(c) Bottle and cup of 'Açana Ware', a variant of Nuzi Ware showing Cretan influence (h. 14 and 11·5 cm). Late 14th century. Açana. (II.I.516)

PLATE 106

106 (a) Ivory inlay depicting a couchant griffin (95 × 38 mm). 14th century B.C. Megiddo. (II.1.41

106 (b) Carved ivory box-lid (h. 3·7 cm): a woman, perhaps a goddess, in a Mycenaean flounced skirt, feeding goats. 14th century B.C. Mīnet el-Beidha. (II.1.512)

106 (c) Ivory plaque (75 × 102 mm) dec ated with a sphinx in high relief. 14th cent B.C. Megiddo. (II.1.513)

PLATE 107

107 (a) Polychrome faience vase in the shape of a woman's head (h. 16 cm). 14th century B.C. Mīnet el-Beidha. (II.1.514) (b) Handle of a walking-stick decorated with the figure of an Asiatic grandee, possibly a caricature of a Mitannian. 18th Dynasty, c. 1355 B.C. Thebes (tomb of Tutankhamun). (II.1.451, 512)

PLATE 108

(a)

(b)

108 (a) Hazor: shrine in Area C, with stelae and seated stone statue. (II.1.537f.) (b) Hazor: temple in Area H. (II.1.536f.)

PLATE 109

(a)

(b)

109   (a) Shechem: Late Bronze Age gate with orthostat jambs.   (II.1.542)   (b) Jericho: Late Bronze Age building in Area H.   (II.1.544)

PLATE 110

110   Jerusalem: stone substructure of Late Bronze Age terraces.   (II.I.546)

PLATE III

111　(a) 'Ammān: Late Bronze Age temple.　(II.1.554)

111　(b) The Palace at Cnossus, Hall of Colonnades at the foot of the Grand Staircase in the domestic quarter.　(II.1.559–60)

PLATE 112

112 (*a*) The Palace at Cnossus, South Propylon. (II.1.565)

112 (*b*) The Viaduct at Cnossus. (II.1.565)

PLATE 113

113   The Stepped Portico, reconstructed, at Cnossus.   (II.1.565)

PLATE 114

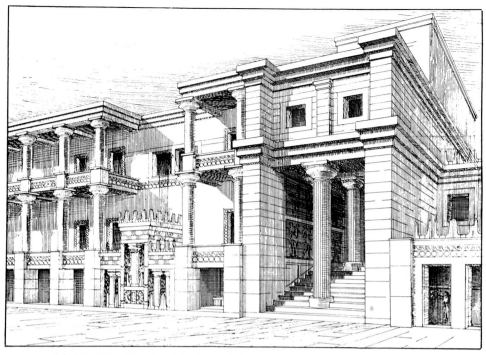

114 (*a*) The West Façade of the Central Court, reconstructed, at Cnossus. (II.1.565)

114 (*b*) Stepped Street. Gournia. (II.1.566)

PLATE 115

115 (a) A royal grave known as the Temple Tomb at Cnossus. (II.1.567)

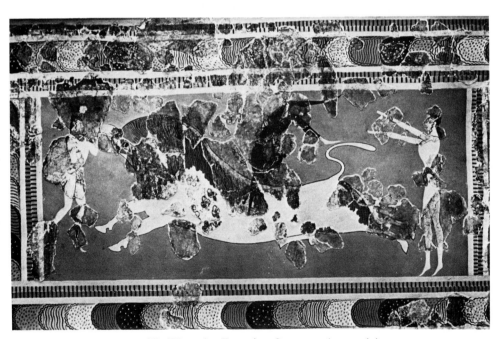

115 (b) 'Toreador Fresco' at Cnossus. (II.1.567)

PLATE 116

116   (a) Keftiu in a fresco painting in the tomb of Merkheperreseneb, Thebes, Egypt.   (II. I . 567, 572)

116   (b) Saffron flowers, in a fresco painting at Hagia Triada in Crete.   (II. I . 568)

PLATE 117

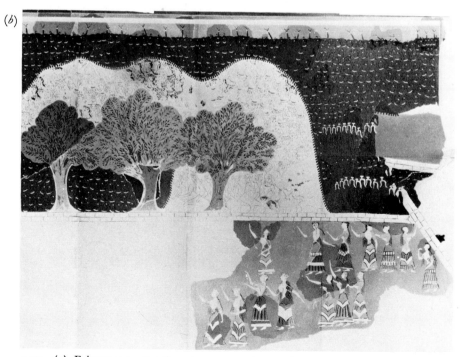

117 (a) Faience statuette of a priestess, sometimes called the 'Snake Goddess'. Cnossus.
(II.1.568) (b) Miniature fresco painting of a religious festival. Cnossus. (II.1.568)

PLATE 118

(a)

(b)

(c)

118 (a) Serpentine goblet, showing foreigners before a high-ranking Minoan. Hagia Triad.
(II.1.568, 572) (b) Late Minoan I vase, decorated with marine motifs; found in Egypt. (II.1.569)
(c) Amphora of the Palace Style. Late Minoan II. (II.1.569)

PLATE 119

(b)

19 (a) Polychrome vase. Late Minoan II. (II.1.569) (b) Amphora of the Palace Style. Late Minoan II. (II.1.569)

PLATE 120

120 (*a*) Minoan gold ring with adoration scene. Beehive tomb near Vaphio, Laconia. (II.I.570)

120 (*b*) Impression taken from a seal with hieroglyphic script. Cnossus. (II.I.570)

120 (*c*) Impression taken from a seal with running lions and palmtree. Zakro. (II.I.570)

PLATE 121

121   Limestone sarcophagus painted with scenes from the cult of the dead. Hagia Triada.   (II.1.576 and II.2.859, 863, 892f.)

PLATE 122

(a)

(b)

122   (a) Cnossus, smaller Throne Room with Griffin fresco. (II.I.579)   (b) Ingots of copper fr
Cyprus, found in a hoard at Hagia Triada.   (II.I.578)

PLATE 123

123　Clay disk covered on both sides with stamped signs, each probably representing a syllable. Undeciphered, but perhaps in a Lycian language. Middle Minoan IIIb. Palace at Phaestus in Crete. (II.1.596)

PLATE 124

124 (*a*) Mask of gold foil (h. *c.* 25 cm), found on the face of the dead man. Mycenae, Shaft Grave V. (II.1.631, 633)

124 (*b*) Grave-stela from Shaft Grave V (h. *c.* 1·30 m). Mycenae. (II.1.631)

124 (*c*) Mycenaean ivory carving, showing a helmet of boar's tusks sewn to a leather cap. L.H. II or III. Delos. (II.1.632)

PLATE 125

125   Bronze daggers, inlaid with gold, silver and niello, (*a*) showing lions, deer and huntsmen, (*b*) showing leopards or panthers chasing wild fowl beside a river. (L. of parts illustrated *c*. 13 cm). Mycenae,
Shaft Grave IV.' (II.1.632)

PLATE 126

126 (*a*) Gold-plated sword-hilt of wood, embossed with patterns of spirals
(l. *c.* 18 cm). Mycenae, Grave Delta. (II.1.631)

126 (*b*) Gold kantharos of Minyan shape (h. 13 cm without handles).
Mycenae, Shaft Grave IV. (II.1.632)

126 (*c*) Crystal vase, probably imported from Egypt (h. *c.* 13 cm).
Mycenae, Grave Omicron. (II.1.632)

PLATE 127

(b)

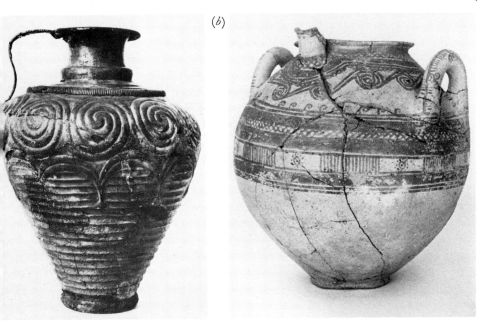

(c)

(d)

27 (a) Silver jug (h. c. 34 cm). Mycenae, Shaft Grave V. (II.1.632) (b) & (c) Matt-painted rs of Mainland type, but (b) decorated with Minoan patterns. Mycenae, Grave Beta. (II.1.633)) Late Helladic I jug with Minoan-style decoration (h. c. 30 cm). Mycenae, Shaft Grave I. .1.633)

PLATE 128

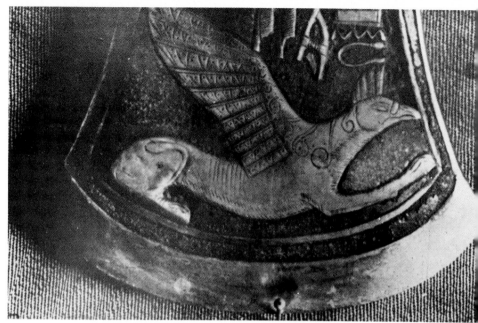

128 (*a*) Copper axe-blade inlaid with gold griffin of Mycenaean type. Tomb of Queen Ahhotp Egypt. (II.1.633–4)

128 (*b*) Fragment of silver rhyton decorated in low relief with siege-scene (actual size). Mycenae, Shaft Grave IV. (II.1.634)

PLATE 129

(b)

129 (a) 'Treasury of Atreus', a *tholos* tomb built in massive blocks of conglomerate stone. Late
Helladic IIIa. Mycenae. (II.1.640) (b) Carved stone ceiling of side chamber of 'Treasury
of Minyas' (*tholos* tomb). Late Helladic II or III. Orchomenus in Boeotia. (II.1.642)

PLATE 130

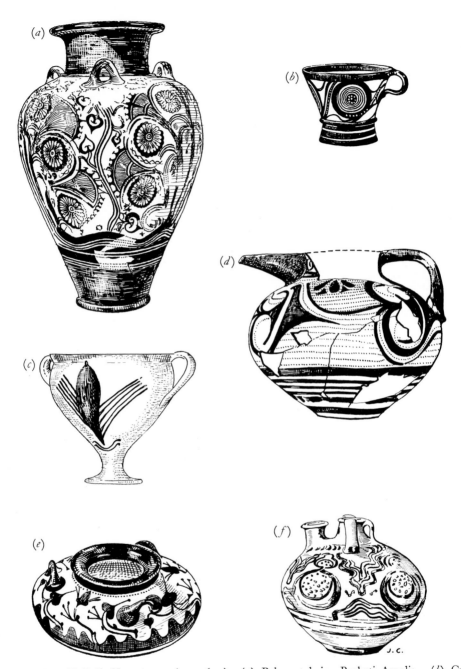

130   Late Helladic II pottery.   (II.I.642)   (*a*) Palace-style jar. Berbati, Argolis.   (*b*) Cup. Prosymna, Argolis.   (*c*) Ephyraean style kylix. Korakou near Corinth.   (*d*) Jug. Chalcis. (*e*) Alabastron. Mycenae.   (*f*) Stirrup-jar. Chalcis.

PLATE 131

131 (*a*) Wall and tower on the eastern side of Troy VI.

131 (*b*) North-eastern angle of the wall of Troy VI.

PLATE 132

(a)

(b)

(c)

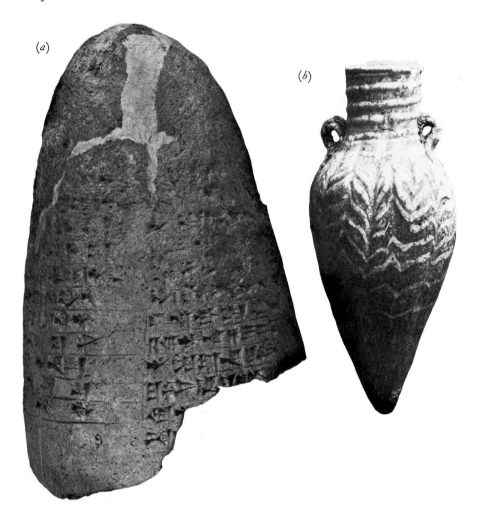

132. (a) Clay cone (h. 24 cm) bearing a *kudurru* inscription: King Kadashman-Enlil I (*c.* 1380 B.C.) confirms a land grant made by his predecessor Kurigalzu I (*c.* 1400 B.C.). (Later *kudurru*s were made of stone: *see* Pls. 161f.).   (II.2.34)   (b) Small bottle (h. 10 cm) of variegated glass of 'Phoenician' type: blue glass with combed pattern in white. 2nd half of 14th century B.C. Ur.   (II.2.44)   (c) Cuneiform tablet (8 × 4 cm), obverse and reverse, containing omens. According to the colophon it was copied in the reign of Meli-Shikhu (1188–1174 B.C.) from an original of Subartu.   (II.2.43)

PLATE 133

(a)

(b)

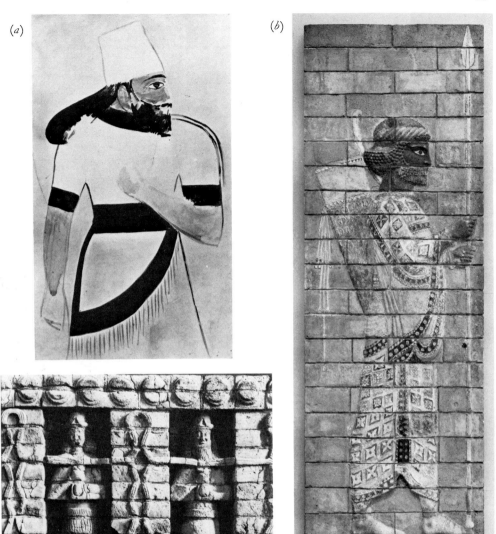

133   (a) Wall-painting (slightly reconstructed) showing a male figure (half life-size), one of a procession decorating the walls of the 'painted Palace' at Dūr-Kurigalzu. 14th century B.C. 'Aqar Quf. (II.2.44)   (b) Figure of an archer in moulded glazed bricks (h. 1·95 m) from a frieze representing the Royal Guard of the Persian kings. c. 500 B.C. Susa (palace of Darius).   (II.2.45)   (c) Deities with 'flowing vase': figures in moulded bricks (h. 2·05 m) in niches on the façade of the temple of Ishtar built by Karaindash, c. 1420 B.C. Uruk.   (II.2.45)

PLATE 134

(a)

(b)

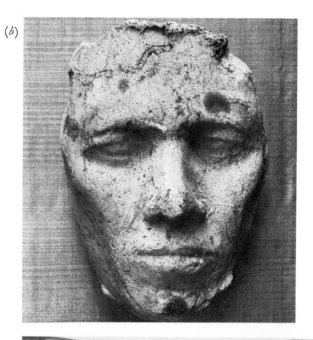

(c)

134 (a) Miniature coffin from the alabaster Canopic chest of Tutankhamun made of solid gold and
inlaid with coloured glass (h. 39·5 cm). 18th Dynasty, c. 1350 B.C. Thebes. (II.2.65) (b) Plaster
mask of an unidentified man, possibly Amenophis III (h. 18 cm). 18th Dynasty, c. 1380 B.C. El-Amarna
(II.2.68) (c) Inner back panel of Tutankhamun's throne, made of wood overlaid with gold and inset
with coloured glass and semiprecious stones (h. 53 cm). See (a). (II.2.66)

PLATE 135

135   (*a*) Limestone relief with figure of Ay and his wife, Tey, receiving a gold collar, one of a number of gifts from the king (w. 43 cm). 18th Dynasty, *c.* 1370 B.C. El-Amarna.   (II.2.70)   (*b*) Mourning scene from a Memphite tomb of the Amarna Period. The future king Horemheb, here given the titles Royal Scribe, Hereditary Prince and Commander of the Army, heads the procession of high officials who follow the two sons of the deceased. 18th Dynasty, *c.* 1360 B.C. Saqqara.   (II.2.71)

PLATE 136

(a)

(b)

(c)

136   (a) Ivory head (h. 16 cm) from a chryselephantine statue of a queen or goddess, with inlaid eyes and curls in gold-and-silver niello work. 14th century B.C. Ras Shamra.   (II.2.135)   (b) Ivory panel (h. 1 m) from a bed-head. It depicts a goddess (perhaps 'Anath) suckling royal twins. 14th century B.C. Ras Shamra.   (II.2.156)   (c) The 'dynastic seal' of Ugarit: a replica of the seal of Yaqaru, son of Niqmaddu, king of Ugarit (early 2nd millennium B.C.) used by all the 14th- and 13th-centuries B.C. kings. Impression on a cuneiform tablet. Ras Shamra.   (II.2.132)

PLATE 137

137   Ugaritian funerary vault. 14th century B.C. Ras Shamra (tomb 1).   (II. 2. 135, 157)

PLATE 138

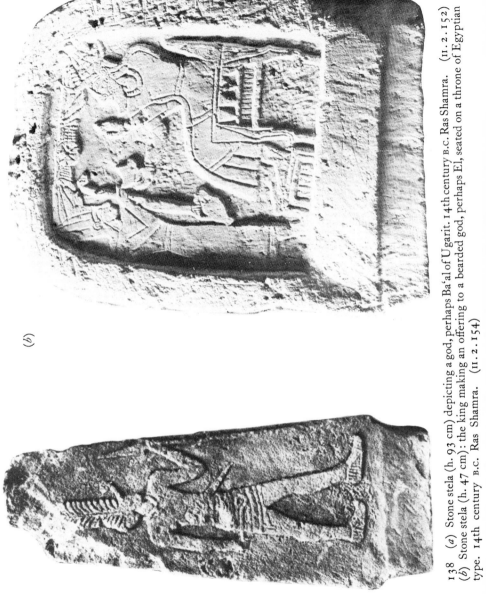

(b)

(a)

138 (a) Stone stela (h. 93 cm) depicting a god, perhaps Baʻal of Ugarit. 14th century B.C. Ras Shamra. (II.2.152)
(b) Stone stela (h. 47 cm): the king making an offering to a bearded god, perhaps El, seated on a throne of Egyptian type. 14th century B.C. Ras Shamra. (II.2.154)

PLATE 139

139 Storage jars in House VII O of Troy VIIa, seen from NW. (11.2.161)

PLATE 140

140   (a) The Lion Gate, entrance to the citadel. Late Helladic IIIb. Mycenae.   (II.2.172)

140   (b) Grave Circle A at Mycenae, enclosing the Shaft Graves. Late Helladic III.
(II.2.172)

PLATE 141

141 (a) Reconstruction of the southern half of the citadel of Tiryns; megaron in centre. Late Helladic III. (II.2.173)

141 (b) Mycenaean palace of Pylus, showing (from foreground) oil-store, megaron with central hearth, ante-room, courtyard. Late Helladic IIIb. (II.2.173)

Plate 142

(a)

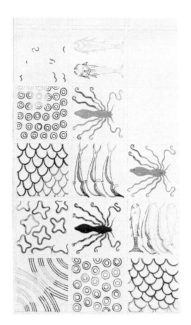

(c)

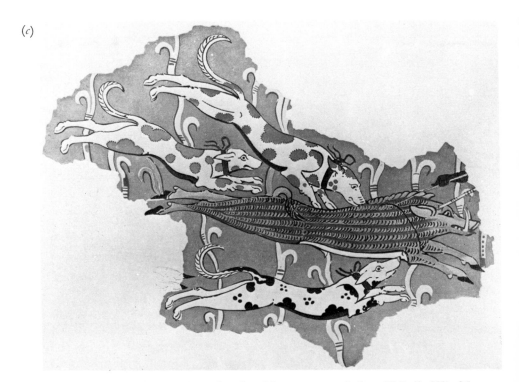

142 (a) Fresco of horses and warriors (h. of figures c. 15 cm). Late Helladic IIIb. Mycenae.
(11.2.174) (b) Painted floor-decoration of fish, octopus, etc. (part). Late Helladic IIIb. Pylus.
(11.2.174) (c) Fresco of boar-hunt (w. c. 43 cm). Late Helladic IIIb. Tiryns. (11.2.174)

PLATE 143

(a)

(b)

143 (a) Ivory statuette-group of two women in Minoan-style dress and a small boy (h. c. 7 cm). Late Helladic II or III. Mycenae. (II.2.175, 879ff.) (b) Miniature ivory columns, perhaps decorations of wooden furniture. Late Helladic III. Mycenae. (II.2.174–5)

PLATE 144

144 Late Helladic III pottery. (II.2.165, 177) (a) Three-handled jar. Rhodes. (b) Tall jug. Attica. (c) Small stirrup-jar. Attica. (d) Piriform stirrup-jar. Rhodes. (e) Ladle. Mycenae. (f) Kylix. Rhodes. (g) Tankard. Attica. (h) Kylix of 'Zygouries' type. (j) Deep bowl. Attica.

PLATE 145

(a)

(b)

(c)

145 (a) Carved stone rhyton (neck and point restored). Late Helladic III. Mycenae. (II.2.175)
b) Carved marble lamp. Late Helladic III. Mycenae.   (II.2.175)   (c) Stone jar. Late Helladic III.
Mycenae.   (II.2.175)

PLATE 146

(a)

(b)

146 (a) Gold cup, with repoussé decoration of octopus etc. (d. c. 18 cm). Late Helladic II. Dendra, Argolis. (II.2.175) (b) Silver bowl inlaid with bull's heads and pomegranate flowers in gold and niello (d. c. 15·9 cm). Late Helladic II or III. Enkomi, Cyprus. (II.2.176, 200)

PLATE 147

(b)

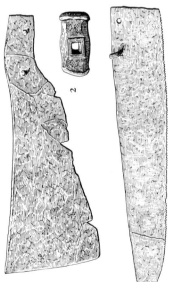

(a)

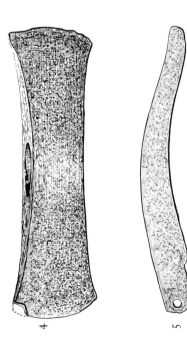

147   (a) Bronze tools: (1) Chopper. Prosymna. (2) Small hammer-head. Mycenae. (3) Saw. Prosymna. (4) Double
axe. Mycenae. (5) Sickle. Mycenae. Late Helladic III.   (II. 2. 176)   (b) Bronze body-armour, from a tomb. Late
Helladic II. Dendra, Argolis.   (II. 2. 176)

PLATE 148

(a)

(b)

(c)

148 (a) Abutment of a Mycenaean bridge. Mycenae. (II.2.180–1). (b) Part of attached column from the façade of the Treasury of Atreus (from a cast). Late Helladic IIIa. Mycenae. (II.2.174, 175) (c) Ivory box and lid carved with griffins and deer (h. c. 16 cm). Late Helladic III. Athens, Agora. (II.2.175, 182)

PLATE 149

149 (a) Pottery *krater* with animal frieze (h. *c.* 35 cm). Late Helladic IIIb. Cyprus. (II.2.182) (b) Cup of local Base-Ring Wareshape, in Mycenaean technique. Late Helladic IIIa. Maroni, Cyprus. (II.2.182) (c) Copper ingot. Late Helladic III. Enkomi, Cyprus. (II.2.182)

PLATE 150

(a)

(b)

150   (a) Pottery vessels of Base-Ring Ware. Late Cypriot I.   (II.2.196)   (b) Pottery vessels
White Slip Ware I and II. Late Cypriot I.   (II.2.196)

PLATE 151

(a)

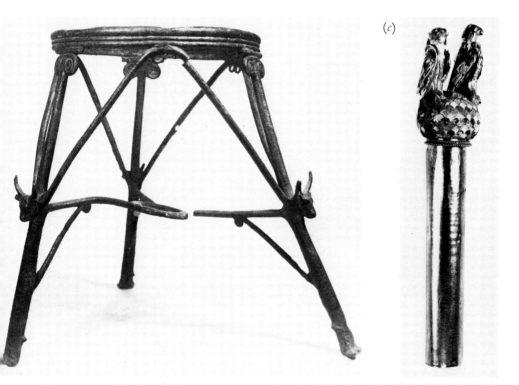

(c)

151 (a) Mycenaean III pictorial *krater*. (11.2.199) (b) Tripod stand with bulls' heads. (c) Sceptre-head of gold and cloisonné work.

PLATE 152

(a)

(b)

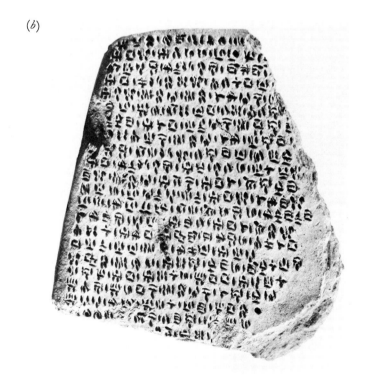

152 (a) Clay tablet inscribed with the signs of a 'Cypro-Minoan' sylla-
bary, undeciphered. 15th-century B.C. Enkomi. (II.1.605–6, II.2.205)
(b) *Ditto.* 13th century B.C. Enkomi. (II.1.606 and II.2.205–6)

PLATE 153

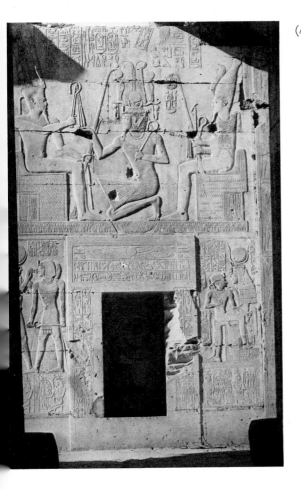

(b)

153 (*a*) Sethos I receives the crook and flail and the emblem for a long reign from Amon-Re (*left*) and Osiris. On one side in the lower scene he sits on the lap of Isis and on the other he receives life and prosperity from Khons. 19th Dynasty, *c*. 1310 B.C. Abydos. (II.2.222, 249) (*b*) Black granite statue of Ramesses II (h. 1·94 m). The small figures on the front of the throne represent Queen Nefertiry and Prince Amenherkhopshef. 19th Dynasty, *c*. 1290 B.C. Karnak. (II.2.249)

PLATE 154

(b)

(a)

154 (a) Central aisle of the Great Hypostyle Hall built by Sethos I and finished by Ramesses II at Karnak. It covers an area of 1¼ acres and its roof is supported by 134 columns. The remains of one of the clerestory windows can be seen above the door at the end. 19th Dynasty, c. 1310 B.C.

(b) Temple-palace of the temple of Ramesses III at Medinet Habu designed to resemble a Syrian *Migdōl*. 20th Dynasty,

PLATE 155

(a)

(c)

155 (a) Wall painting from the tomb of Nefertiry, principal wife of Ramesses II. Isis leads the queen by the hand. 19th Dynasty, c. 1275 B.C. Thebes. (II.2.250) (b) Assyrian stone symbol-base (h. 1·05 m): Tukulti-Ninurta I (1244–1208 B.C.) stands between two men holding sun-standards. Ashur. (II.2.305f.) (c) Assyrian stone symbol-base (h. 57·5 cm) dedicated by Tukulti-Ninurta I (1244–1208 B.C.) to the god Nusku. The king appears twice, standing and kneeling before a similar symbol-base. Ashur. (II.2.305f., 480)

PLATE 156

(a)

(c)

(b)

(d)

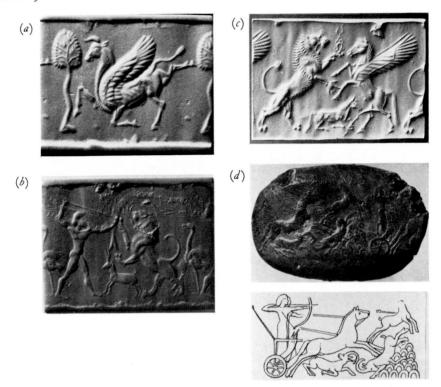

(e)

156   (a)–(c) Impressions from Assyrian cylinder seals: (a) a winged bull in front of a tree (h. 31 m
d. 12 mm); (b) a naked hero attacking a lion with a spear (h. 45 mm, d. 18 mm); (c) a fight betwe
a lion and a winged horse (h. 41 mm, d. 16 mm). 13th century B.C.   (II.2.304, 481)   (d) Clay tab
impressed with the seal of Ninurta-tukulti-Ashur (c. 1150 B.C.), depicting the king on a chariot hunt
ibexes on high ground. (Original, and drawing showing the scene in its proper sequence.) Ash
(II.2.481)   (e) General view of the site of Chogha Zanbil. *In the centre:* the zikkurrat, seen from S
Left of zikkurrat: temples of Ishmekarab, Kiririsha and *GAL*; *right:* temples of Naprate, Shimut a
NIN.URU, Ada and Shala, and Pinikir. *Top left:* temples of Hishmetik and Ruhuratir.   (II.2.3

PLATE 157

(b)

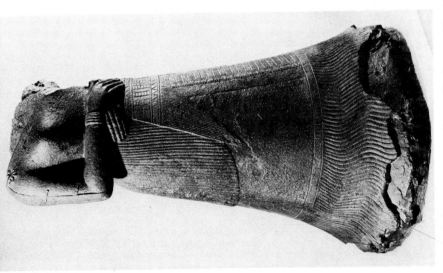

(a)

157 (a) Bronze statue of Queen Napirasu, wife of Untash-(d)GAL (c. 1274–1255 B.C.). The headless figure is 1·20 m high and weighs 1,750 kg. (II. 2. 399, 497) (b) The so-called Midas Monument: a façade cut in the rock (h. 16·9 m). The inscription, in Phrygian, mentions King Midas. 6th century B.C. Yazilikaya near Eskişehir. (II. 2. 419, 437)

PLATE 158

(a)

(b)

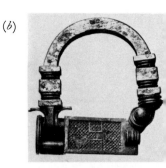

(c)

158 (a) Painted pottery jug (h. 10·5 cm) decorated with animal figures and geometric pattern. Middl
Phrygian style, 8th century B.C. Gordion (tumulus of the Princess). (II.2.427) (b) Three of the 1
Phrygian bronze fibulae found in the Great Tumulus at Gordion. 8th century B.C. (II.2.42
(c) Bronze bowl with ring-handle and ladle. 8th century B.C. Gordion. (II.2.428)

PLATE 159

(*b*)

(*c*)　　　　　(*d*)

59　(*a*) Rock-relief at Ivriz near Konya. Detail showing King Urpalla (*c.* 720 B.C.) wearing a fibula of the type illustrated on Pl. 158(*b*).　(II.2.428, 431)　(*b*) Drawing of a wall-relief of Sargon of Assyria (721–705 B.C.) showing Phrygian tributaries. The first one wears a large bow-shaped fibula. Khorsabad.　(II.2.428)　(*c*) Stone statue (h. 1·34 m) of the goddess Cybele flanked by two youths playing the double flute and the lyre. 6th century B.C. Boğazköy.　(II.2.432)　(*d*) Stone relief depicting Cybele in a shrine (h. 1·75 m).　(II.2.433)

PLATE 160

160   Gordion: the outer wall. 8th century B.C.   (II.2.430)

PLATE 161

(b)

(a)

161 (a) Boundary stone (*kudurru*) (h. 90 cm) of Meli-Shikhu (1188–1174 B.C.). The king is shown introducing his daughter to the goddess Nanā. Susa. (II. 2. 445) (b) Boundary stone (*kudurru*) (h. 64·5 cm) of Nebuchadrezzar I (1124–1103 B.C.), decorated with divine symbols. Abu Ḥabbah. (II. 2. 455)

PLATE 162

162 (*a*) The so-called 'Broken Obelisk' (h. 61 cm) inscribed with royal annals possibly in the reign of Ashur-bēl-kala (1074–1057 B.C.). The relief represents the king facing captive enemies. Nineveh (II.2.467, 480)   (*b*) Eight-sided clay prism inscribed with the annals of Tiglath-pileser I (1115–1077 B.C.). This is the text selected by the Royal Asiatic Society in 1857 to test the validity of the decipherment of the cuneiform script. Ashur.   (II.2.457)   (*c*) Boundary stone (*kudurru*) (h. 60 cm) of Marduk-nādin-ahhē (1098–1081 B.C.) showing the standing figure of the king.   (II.2.461)

PLATE 163

(a)

163 (a) The High Priest Amenhotpe receives rewards from Ramesses IX. Two courtiers have put a gold collar on his neck and other gifts are placed between him and the king. In accordance with an artistic convention the size of a representation is related to the importance of the person represented. 20th Dynasty, c. 1130 B.C. Temple of Amun, Karnak. (II.2.628–9). (b) Hrihor presents bouquets to Amun whose wife, Amunet, is also shown. 20th Dynasty, c. 1100 B.C. Temple of Khons, Karnak. (II.2.638)

PLATE 164

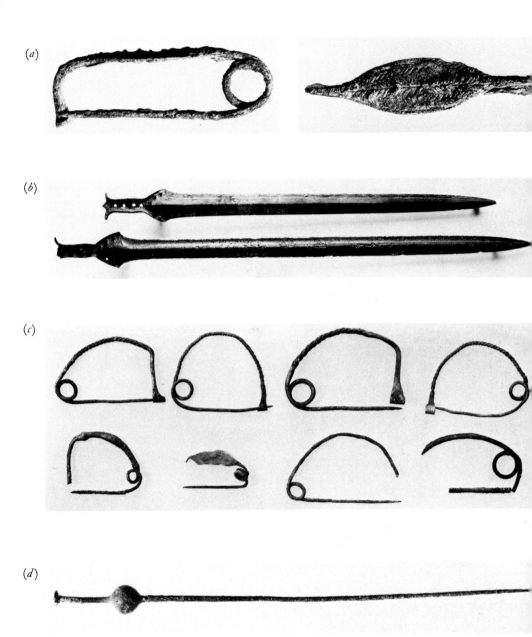

164 (a) Violin-bow fibula. L.H. IIIc. Perati. (II.2.662) (b) Naue II swords. L.H. III b–c. Kall thea (Achaea). (II.2.662) (c) Arched fibulae. Submycenaean. Ceramicus, Athens. (II.2.664) (d) Dress pin. Submycenaean. Unknown provenance. (II.2.664)

PLATE 165

165 L.H. IIIc Close Style. (11.2.662) (a) Trefoil-lipped oinochoe. Mycenae. (b) Stirrup jar. Mycenae. (c) Stirrup jar. Asine.

PLATE 166

166 L.H. IIIc Octopus Style stirrup jars
(11.2.663) (*a*) Perati. (*b*) Naxos. (*c*) Co

PLATE 167

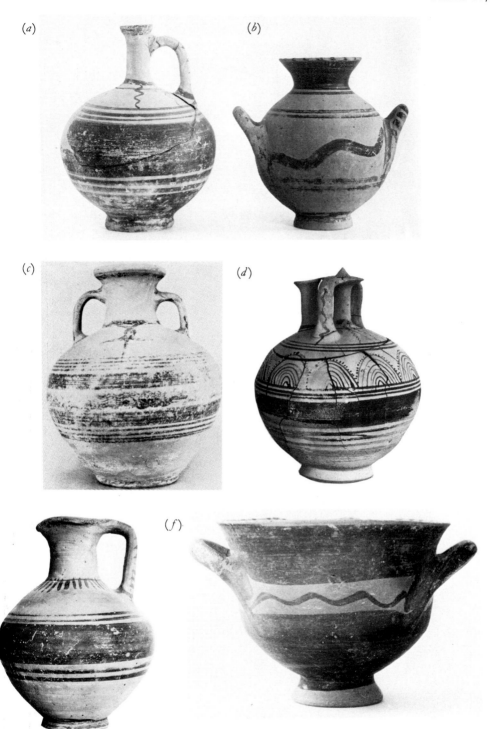

(a)   (b)

(c)   (d)

(f)

67   Submycenaean vases.   (II.2.664)   (a) Lekythos. Ceramicus, Athens.   (b) Amphoriskos. Cera-
icus, Athens.   (c) Neck-handled amphora. Ceramicus, Athens.   (d) Stirrup jar. Ceramicus, Athens.
•) Trefoil-lipped oinochoe. Ceramicus, Athens.   (f) Bowl. Lefkandi, Euboea.

PLATE 168

(a)

(b)

168   (a) Pyxis. L.H. IIIc. Lefkandi, Euboea.   (II.2.
666)   (b) Helmet. Submycenaean. Tiryns.   (II.2.671)

PLATE 169

169 Protogeometric vases from Athens. (ii. 2. 672) (a) Trefoil-lipped oinochoe. Ceramicus. (b) Belly-handled amphora. Nea Ionia. (c) Neck-handled amphora. Nea Ionia. (d) Skyphos. Ceramicus. (e) Lekythos. Ceramicus.

PLATE 170

(a)

(b)

170   (a) Goddess. L.M. IIIc–Subminoan. Karphi.   (II.2.676)   (b) Centaur. c. 900 B.C. Lefkan
Euboea.   (II.2.674)

PLATE 171

(a)   (b)   (d)

171   Sub-Minoan vases from Cnossus.   (II.2.677)   (a) Stirrup jar.   (b) Trefoil-lipped oinochoe.
(c) Stirrup jar.   (d) Belly-handled amphora.

PLATE 172

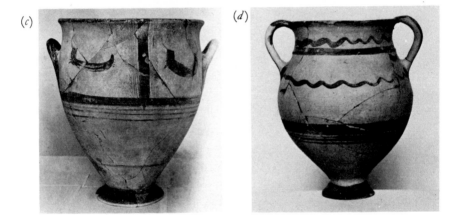

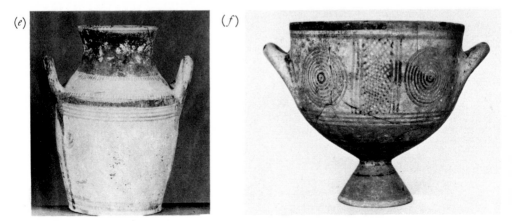

172 Protogeometric vases from Cnossus. (II.2.677) (a) Neck-handled amphora. (b) Stirrup jar.
(c) Bell krater. (d) Krateriskos. (e) Pyxis. (f) Skyphos (Attic import).

PLATE 173

173 (*a*) Spiral patterns carved in relief in the Tarxien Temples. Malta. (II.2.731) (*b*) Spiral patterns painted on a ceiling in the Hal Saflieni Hypogeum. Malta. (II.2.731) (*c*) Façade of rock-cut tomb with carved pilasters. Castelluccio culture. South-east Sicily, Cava Lazzara cemetery. (II.2.732)

PLATE 174

(a)

(b)

174 (a) Huts of the Bronze Age village at Punta Milazzese, Panarea (Lipari islands), type-site of the Milazzese culture. Middle Bronze Age. (I.2.733) (b) Nuraghe Su Nuraxis, Barumini, Sardinia, seen from the south. (II.2.739)

PLATE 175

(a) (b) (d)

75 (a) Bronze figurine of the Nuraghic period in Sardinia, showing a warrior with four eyes and
ur arms. Teti, Abini. (11.2.741) (b) Bronze figurine of the Nuraghic period in Sardinia, showing
woman holding a dead man. Urzulei, Nuoro. (11.2.741) (c) The *Dama de Elche*, head of an
berian statue. (11.2.767) (d) *Têtes coupées*, from Entremont, south France. (11.2.756)

PLATE 176

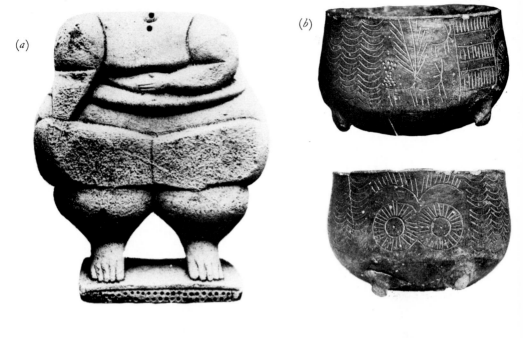

176 (a) Statue of standing 'divine' figure of limestone from the Haġar Qim Temples, Mal[
(II.2.730) (b) Vase with symbolic pattern, from Los Millares. (II.2.761) (c) Bronze sit[
from an Etruscan burial vault at the cemetery of Certosa. 5th century B.C. (II.2.722)

PLATE 177

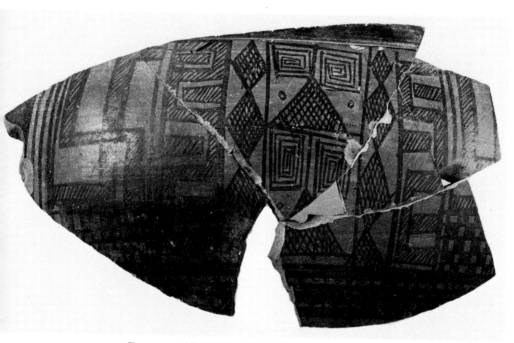

177   Fragment of Ionic Geometric vase at Smyrna.   (II.2.785)

PLATE 178

(a)

(c)

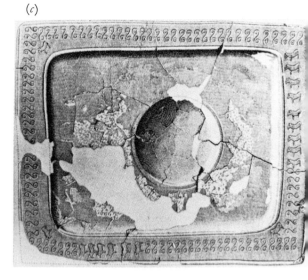

(b)

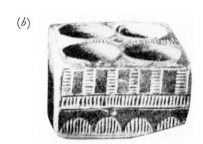

(d)

178   (a) Gold ring from Thebes, showing an altar.   (b) Stone receptacle with four depressions in the top. Kumasa, in Crete.   (II.2.859)   (c) Offering table in the Middle Minoan shrine at Phaestu (II.2.859)   (d) Double axes on top of *bucrania*. On an amphora from Pseira, Crete.   (II.2.86 (e) Pier with double axes incised on its blocks. Cnossus.   (II.2.864)

PLATE 179

(b)

179   Snake goddesses from Cnossus: (a) in faience, (b) in gold and ivory.   (ii.2.867)

179   (c) Sacrificial scene from the Hagia Triada sarcophagus.   (ii.2.872f.)

PLATE 180

(a)

(b)

(c)

(d)

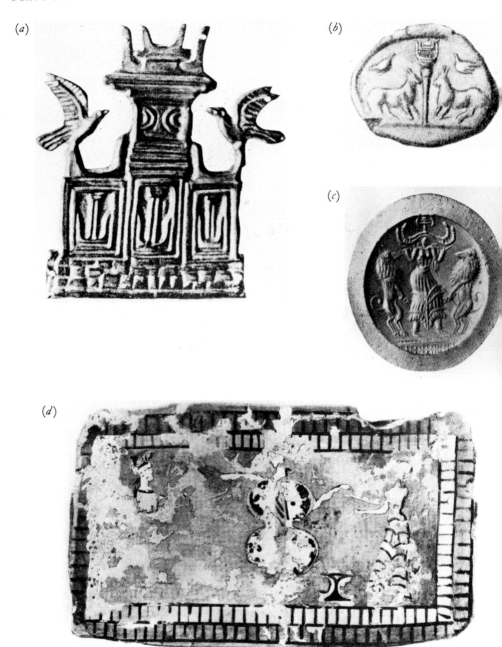

180 (a) Model of a shrine with horns of consecration and birds. Mycenae. (II.2.877) (b) Co
with horns of consecration and animals, on an impression taken from a seal at Mycenae. (II.2.
(c) Seal-stone showing goddess with double axe on her head. Mycenae. (II.2.878) (d) Goddes
shield; painted limestone plaque. Mycenae. (II.2.878)

PLATE 181

181   Zeus with the scales of destiny, on a Mycenaean vase. Enkomi, Cyprus.   (II.2.884)